Training and Fighting Skills

by World Champion Benny 'The Jet' Urquidez

with Émil Farkas and Stuart Sobel

UNIQUE PUBLICATIONS

Assisting Benny Urquidez is Dale Jacoby

Graphic Design/Tim Chapman
Cover Photo/Robert Reiff
Interior Photos/Ed Ikuta, Dave King, Stuart Sobel

© **UNIQUE PUBLICATIONS, INC., 1981**
Printed in the United States of America
ISBN No.: 0-86568-015-9
Library of Congress No.: 80-54831

DEDICATION

I give the glory to the Lord and the dedication to my family. To my inspiration, my wife Sara and daughter Monique, who make it all worthwhile. To my mother, who always believed in me and my talents and never let me down. To my brother Arnold, the finest trainer in the world, who brought these talents out. To my brothers Ruben, Smiley, Blinky, Mando, Manuel and my sister Lily who went through it all with me.

I would also like to give a special thanks and a sincere word of appreciation to my first instructor Bill Ryusaki, who gave me much needed encouragement and consideration when I first began my martial arts training at the age of eight. I have not forgotten.

CONTENTS

FOREWORD

Martial arts are generally thought of in terms of a style or system which is loyally supported with the same fervor given to a fraternal organization. Full-contact karate does not claim any one style. Rather it gives credit to all of the fighting arts for its application. Through this sport, new techniques in training and competition have surfaced by modifying many of our traditional methods.

Being the pioneer in any sport always means traveling a path full of pitfalls. The men to meet this challenge were few in number. They came primarily from the ranks of traditional karate, trying to fill the void of competitors. Some succeeded. Most didn't.

When the history books are written about these early men and women of full-contact karate there will be a special place of honor given to Benny Urquidez. He has bridged that chasm between amateur and professional and by doing so blazed a trail for others to follow.

Nicknamed "The Jet" because of his quick effective style, this versatile champion has traveled the world competing with the best that a country had to offer. He has bested the best in their own home towns, playing by their own rules. But perhaps just as important, he has not only made many new friends during his travels, but many new converts to the sport as well.

Benny "The Jet" fights like a champion, but just as notable, he also has the attitude of a champion. The Champ looks upon the entire matter of competition as exciting, enlightening and an exercise in mental strategy as well as physical ability.

After numerous requests by his legion of fans to write the first book on his training and competing techniques, he has finally agreed. But where do you begin?

Over the many years that Benny Urquidez has taught the martial arts and the thousands of students that have learned from him, he has noted a similarity in the questions that were asked. They seem to be universal, with each step of training bringing forth new problems to solve in the mind of the student.

He has taken the most frequently asked questions and answered them for all to understand. The questions have been separated into the chapter headings that divide the book. It is hoped that this method will enhance your learning experience.

Benny Urquidez was a champion competitor in the traditional arts for over 14 years. All of the techniques he uses in the ring are credited to their origin in the martial arts. For that reason this book is perfect not only for the karate practitioner and the tournament fighter, but also for the full-contact competitor. Everything you see in this book has been tried and proven in actual competition. It works for him, it works for his students. With practice and a desire to be the best, it will work for you as well.

Stuart Sobel
Emil Farkas

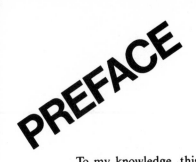

PREFACE

To my knowledge, this is the first book on professional full-contact karate. The overwhelming number of requests for me to put my thoughts and techniques down on paper prompted me to pass on to you the knowledge and methods which have made me the competitor I am today.

When full contact first began as a sport in the United States in the early seventies, few saw any future in it. Many saw it as detrimental to traditional karate. I felt just the opposite. Here was a sport that could open up new vistas, allow the martial artist freedom to explore new methods and combine them with already established techniques for a better, more practical form of combat. I also realized that unlike boxing, traditional karate had no mass audience appeal because it was all based on techniques pulled short of the target. It was extremely difficult to follow, except for the trained eye. I felt that with full contact, a whole new world would open up which would benefit the traditionalist as well as the experimentalist.

As the sport grew and became recognized, one drawback became apparent. Few fighters were ready to step into the professional ring. Those who tried soon discovered that full-contact karate was unlike its nonprofessional counterpart. An even larger problem was that few trainers were available to teach these upcoming fighters the proper methods of full-contact fighting.

That is the major reason for this book. I have been fortunate in having the best coach from the very beginning, my brother Arnold Urquidez, and in being given the freedom to experiment with my own ideas. Through dedication and hard work, I reached the top in the sport. Now I want to take this knowledge and pass it on to you.

My major objective is not to discard the traditional arts. They are my foundation. I want to expand the minds of all of you who are ready to learn. I want to show you that there are modified methods that can and do work. The key is to learn to adapt yourself to your situation and flow with it. Don't restrict yourself. If I can accomplish this for you, then I will have done my share in the growth of the sport. I sincerely hope, as you read through these pages, that you will go with what I am saying and take it as far as you can. You're only limited by the goals you set.

Benny Urquidez

SPEED

IS SPEED THE MOST IMPORTANT OVERALL DEVELOPMENT FOR KARATE COMPETITION?

Yes. For both offensive and defensive techniques you must have speed. Your reaction time must be quick in order to get in and out. Speed requires quick reaction time and strength to push and pull your body and your weapons.

IS IT EASIER TO DEVELOP SPEED IN YOUR HANDS OR YOUR FEET?

It is easier to develop speed in your hands because you don't carry as much weight.

HOW DO YOU WORK ON DEVELOPING YOUR REFLEXES?

There is only one way to develop your reflexes and that is through repetition. Initially , you have to mentally train an action until it becomes just that, a reflex. You develop it through repetition.

CAN YOU TRAIN TO MAKE DISTANCING A WEAPON IN ITSELF?

Distancing can be a weapon, but not by itself of course. You would first test your opponent with, let's say, a feint. You see if your opponent moves back or stays put. If he moves back more than once in reaction to your feint, then you can be pretty certain that he always will because that is how he has trained. I always say that the way you train is the way you react. Knowing this bit of information you can create distance between you and him with a feint, thereby setting him up for a jump kick or other long range technique.

IS SPEED RELATED TO SIZE?

Usually the smaller person has the advantage because he is closer to the ground and can maneuver more quickly. The taller person, because of his farther distance to the ground and his actual physical weight, would be slower than his smaller counterpart.

POWER

WHERE DOES POWER COME FROM?

Power starts from the center of the gut. You can develop power with equipment, such as weights and bags, but the most important kind of power is mental discipline. You've heard, I'm sure, of some people who are incredibly strong when they were in some kind of panic situation. It's not that they've trained for it, it is just that their mental powers took over and they were able to do things that they never considered doing before. A person can train his mind as well as his body, but the mind and the attitude have to be right before a person can develop power.

DO YOU THINK POWER IS NECESSARY FOR FIGHTING?

You definitely have got to have power in your hands, legs, gut and mind to be an effective fighter.

WHAT IS THE DIFFERENCE BETWEEN POWER AND STRENGTH?

People who have power are not necessarily strong. Strength comes internally. Power comes more from the outside of the body.

WHAT IS THE DIFFERENCE BETWEEN NAUTILUS AND BARBELL WORK-OUTS?

Nautilus equipment works against your own power and strength. Barbells are dead weights that work against gravity. Nautilus builds inner strength. Barbells build outer strength and bulk, which could have a tendency to shorten your reach.

HOW CAN A PERSON STRENGTHEN THE WRISTS?

There are many good exercises that are available. Some of the more popular ones are squeezing a ball or squeezing vise grips which use a spring for tension. This is one of the times you can use a barbell or dumbbells. Hold them at a 90 degree angle and move your wrists up and down.

WILL DYNAMIC TENSION EXERCISES INCREASE STRENGTH?

I believe that dynamic tension is the best kind of strengthening exercise that a person can do. The reason for this is because you are not pushing with more than your strength nor less than your strength. You are pushing against your own limitations. So as you become stronger, the tension increases.

IS HIP ROTATION IMPORTANT IN GIVING YOU POWER?

Yes, hip rotation is very important. However, it is best utilized if, rather than going into a locked position, it goes past that position of locking. Hip rotation is important for combinations.

WHAT IS MORE POWERFUL, HANDS OR FEET?

Naturally the feet are more powerful because they are heavier. The muscles are bigger and the femur bone in the thigh is the largest bone in the body.

CAN A SMALLER GUY BE AS POWERFUL AS A BIGGER GUY?

Yes, definitely. It is not so much the outer bulk but the inner strength that is important. Then we're talking about leverage.

TIMING

WHAT IS YOUR DEFINITION OF TIMING?

Timing means meeting your object with a certain technique that will reach maximum speed at the moment of impact.

IS THERE EQUIPMENT WHICH CAN BE USED TO LEARN TIMING?

The timing bag and speed bag are used to learn timing. You can learn timing through pacing yourself when you skip rope and when you run.

HOW IMPORTANT IS TIMING IN KARATE?

Timing is very important. If you get a big person who isn't very quick, he depends on timing. A smaller person who is very quick doesn't rely on timing as much. He relies more on speed. It is actually very important for any fighter, but a bigger person is more dependent on it.

WHAT IS RHYTHM?

Rhythm works on a beat and motion. It is a continuing steady pace, a measured motion.

WHAT IS EYE GAP?

Using your eye and your opponent to judge the distance in which to use your weapons.

WILL CONSTANT REPETITION IMPROVE TIMING?

Yes. Any time you use a technique in a repetitive manner, timing will automatically come. It will happen naturally.

WHAT IS THE DIFFERENCE BETWEEN REFLEX AND TIMING?

Reflex is a spontaneous reaction process, not a thinking one. It happens automatically. You have to work on timing to perfect it. Timing you have to see.

ARE BLOCKING AND TIMING INTERRELATED?

Definitely. You have to have your timing down to either avoid or redirect your opponent's weapons.

DO YOU THINK USING MUSIC DURING WORK-OUTS IS BENEFICIAL?

Not only is it beneficial, it is also more enjoyable. It can give you that rhythm and beat that you need.

WHY IS SPARRING THE BEST WAY TO DEVELOP GOOD TIMING?

Sparring is the best because you're doing it for real. You have an object kicking and striking back at you. So you are under pressure to pay attention and not let your mind wander.

TARGET AREAS

WHAT ARE THE MAIN TARGETS IN PROFESSIONAL KARATE?

In competition, the target areas above the waist run in a vertical line known as the main line. Starting with the top of the head, the nose, the jaw, the throat, the collar bone, solar plexus, the gut and the bladder. Off to the side parallel to the main line there is a target area just underneath the heart. Going horizontally across the mid-section there are the bladder, liver and kidneys. Below the waist there are the thighs and calves. No joint, groin, or spine techniques allowed.

WHAT ABOUT THE TARGET AREAS IN A REAL FIGHT?

In a real fight the main target areas are the weakest points such as the bridge of the nose, the temple, behind the ear, the throat, the groin, the spine, and any strike against the joints. Of course, you can also include the main target areas you would use in the ring.

ARE THERE ANY TARGET AREAS THAT ARE OFF-LIMITS IN AMERICAN FULL CONTACT?

Yes. You are not allowed to strike the groin, the throat, the spine, against the joints and to use any techniques which include down blows.

IS IT NECESSARY TO ALWAYS ATTACK A SPECIFIC TARGET?

Yes. The best target to hit constantly is the body, because the body continually weakens. There is an old saying that if you hit the body the head will follow. If you continue hitting the same area over and over you will eventually weaken it and do damage as well.

WHAT DOES SHARP SHOOTING MEAN?

Sharp shooting is used in training. Do not use your techniques with full power. Instead, concentrate on forcing your opponent to make an opening so you can aim a technique to whatever area you want. It is strictly a training device. You do this without getting hit. This way you can work on your speed, timing and repetition.

WHAT IS THE MOST FRAGILE PART OF THE BODY?

In my opinion, it is the throat.

STRATEGY

WHAT DO YOU DO THE FIRST TIME YOU MEET YOUR OPPONENT IN THE RING?

In the ring, I really get to know my opponent. During the first round, I test his weapons, determining his strongest and weakest points. In the second round, I test his body. I see if he can take punishment, see if he has a good jaw and if his legs are in good condition. It's in the third round that I start going for his weak points.

WHY DO YOU WAIT UNTIL THE THIRD ROUND BEFORE GOING AFTER YOUR OPPONENT'S WEAK POINTS? ISN'T THIS ALMOST TOO LATE IF HE IS AGGRESSIVE?

Usually it is a way of testing your opponent's skills. A professional, however, never waits for the third round. He can generally tell what his opponent is like after the first round. Speaking strictly for myself, this is the way I start off. The three rounds are a warm-up for me, but I wouldn't advise waiting that long for anybody else. Since an amateur only has three rounds, he had better figure out his opponent's tactics in the first round.

HOW DO YOU DECIDE WHAT LEAD MOVE TO USE WHEN YOU CLOSE THE GAP?

Generally you would use your front hand because it's closer to your opponent and it gets in quicker. With your front hand you cover his eyes with a jab and then follow up with a kick, punch, throw or clinch.

HOW DO YOU DEAL WITH AN OPPONENT WHO IS AN IN-FIGHTER?

Learn to use your front hands as a jab to cover his eyes and use your legs as a jab as well to make him keep his distance. If he comes in on you too fast, learn to tie up his hands in a clinch.

HOW DO YOU DEAL WITH AN OPPONENT WHO IS ALWAYS DANCING AWAY?

You learn how to cut the corners. An example would be if he is at 12:00 and he dances clockwise, you meet him by going in a straight line to 3:00. If he dances counterclockwise you meet him by going in a straight line to 9:00.

HOW DO YOU DETERMINE YOUR OPPONENT'S WEAK POINTS?

First, you have to test his weapons. You see how fast they are, how accurate they are and how much power they have behind them. If he has good hands you try to pick away at his weaker points, such as the kidneys, the liver, etc., by using your legs. If he has good legs you have to smother them by getting in close and then working on his body. You test his weapons when they hit your block so you never have to take the full impact to know what your opponent has to dish out.

HOW DO YOU GET YOUR OPPONENT TO MAKE A MISTAKE?

You test him. Test his reaction. Anybody that trains has a habit of doing certain things during his training. The way you train is the way you react. You test him with a fake or a feint and see if he moves back. If he reacts that way more than once then you know that is the way he has trained and he will react that way again. If he opens a gap for you in a reaction to your move, then you can place him where you want him.

DO YOU CHANGE YOUR STRATEGY FOR OPPONENTS WHO ARE MUCH LARGER, SMALLER OR THE SAME SIZE AS YOU ARE?

The strategy is always mental. Physically, I fight them all the same. If you fight a big guy you fight him hard and to the inside. If you fight a smaller guy you fight him hard to the outside. When I say you fight them all the same I mean you hit them all hard and you hit the same spots, ie., liver, kidneys, etc. Somebody big should be fought to his inside because he has the advantage of distance over you and can hit you. You have to be on his inside to smother his weapons so he can't use that reach against you. A smaller guy moves just as quickly as you, theoretically, so you want to stay away from his weapons by keeping to his outside.

HOW IMPORTANT IS IT TO "PSYCH OUT" YOUR OPPONENT?

Very important. You begin by psyching your opponent out mentally. You do this by the way you look at him, your expressions, your attitude, your self-assurance, your enthusiasm, your charisma. They are all very important. Then you work on him verbally. You can tell him, "We're going to give the audience a good show. We're going to let them know we came here to fight." There are ways of making him doubt his own ability.

To physically intimidate your opponent, you might hit his glove in the beginning of each round with a strong solid tap, showing him the strength in your hands. You might also stomp the ground hard for the noise effect. You could tighten up your muscles and look him straight in the eyes. Try poking him with your thumb in the solar plexus and say with a slight smile and perhaps a wink, "Good luck" after the referee's instructions. Or you give him a pat on the shoulder with a sturdy closed fit and then say to him, "We're going to have a good fight." I've seen men melt before the first round with techniques like these.

DO YOU BELIEVE IN SCOUTING YOUR OPPONENT, SUCH AS FINDING OUT WHERE HE TRAINS, VIEWING HIS OTHER FIGHTS, OR FINDING OUT ANY OTHER INFORMATION ABOUT HIM?

No. There is no need for that. He'll never fight the same way in the ring, because he'll react differently to the way you react. It is good to know if he has good legs or hands because it makes you aware of them. If you study a film he could fool you by reversing his tactics and then you can be all messed up. You see, if you have to think about what you're doing, it's too late. You don't have time to think, you only have time to react. So what you do is react to his motion, not to what you think he's going to do.

DO YOU CHOOSE A SPARRING PARTNER FOR A SPECIFIC BOUT?

Usually I get three or four different sparring partners with different weights and speeds. Some of them are about my size and are very quick. They will keep me quick. Then I will get some a little heavier and slower, but who hit a lot harder. That way I get to feel different power levels and strength as well as speed.

DOES YOUR CORNER MAN GIVE YOU STRATEGY DURING THE FIGHT?

No. If my corner man has to tell me how to fight my opponent, then I don't belong in the ring. The thing my corner man does is to make me aware of what my opponent is doing to me. He'll say, for example, "This guy is catching you with a round kick to the head on your right side." That could only mean that my right hand is low.

If he tells me, "This guy is catching you with a jab," that could only mean that my left hand must be low and that I'm not moving my head. He makes me aware for two reasons. One is to help me make a better defense and the other is to make me aware of an opening that I might not have seen.

NUTRITION

WHAT ARE THE BEST FOODS TO EAT?

Seafood, poultry and liver. Turkey is also very good since it is easy to digest and terrific if you want to lose weight.

IS IT NECESSARY TO EAT THREE TIMES A DAY?

In my opinion, no. Twice a day is sufficient. Usually a good breakfast between seven and eight in the morning and a good dinner no later than six in the evening is the ideal schedule.

HOW MUCH SHOULD YOU EAT?

You should eat only as much as your stomach will hold. Most of us keep eating even though we are satisfied. Learn to push the plate away when you are full. Your appetite will decrease and you'll feel better and be able to have better workouts.

SHOULD YOU REST AFTER EATING?

If that means going to sleep or just sitting down the answer is no. You should take a walk after every meal. It will help your body digest the food and will prevent the meal from turning into fat.

DO YOU RECOMMEND VITAMINS?

Vitamins are necessary to supplement your body's needs, especially since you expend more energy in a short amount of time than the average individual. To allow your body to perform well under this extra effort you must replace the vitamins which burn up quickly during workouts.

WHAT TYPE OF VITAMINS DO YOU RECOMMEND?

A basic vitamin program should include B complex, C and E.   The B complex helps with the energy that is burned up. The C fights off germs, especially when you are sweating and your pores are open. B15 is another good vitamin to take. It supplies more oxygen to the blood stream, thus giving you more endurance. Cayenne (red pepper) in capsule form will also speed up your blood circulation.

IS IT DETRIMENTAL TO EAT AND WORK OUT?

I think so. After eating you should walk to burn off some calories and to help your body digest the food. You must give your body plenty of time to digest the food in your stomach. Don't do any hard exercise for at least two hours after eating.

IS JUNK FOOD REALLY UNHEALTHY?

There are some people who live on junk food and they do fine. But I think for most people junk food all the time is not good. I know sometimes my body yearns for things like sugar and salt. What I do is treat myself on Sunday and call it my "junk day." I treat myself to any type of food that I want, but the rest of the week, I stay away from these foods.

WHEN YOU ARE THIRSTY SHOULD YOU DRINK WARM OR COLD LIQUIDS?

Believe it or not, warm liquids quench the thirst better than cold liquids. With warm liquids, a little will do the job. It's not good to drink a lot when you are thirsty. Cold liquids will fill you, but won't quench the thirst as quickly.

CONDITIONING

HOW DO YOU RUN?

There are different patterns in running. When you first begin to run the mile you will run a half mile, walk a quarter mile and sprint a quarter mile. Do this for two weeks. For running the second mile, run the first mile, then walk a quarter mile, sprint a quarter mile, walk a quarter mile and sprint a quarter mile. The maximum you need to run is six miles. When you work up to that you will run for five miles then walk a quarter mile, sprint a quarter mile, walk a quarter mile, and sprint the final quarter mile. Walk at a fast pace.

IS THERE ANY SPECIAL EQUIPMENT YOU NEED TO RUN?

In addition to good running shoes, you will need a mouthpiece to train you to breathe through your nose.

WHY SHOULD YOU BREATHE THROUGH YOUR NOSE?

Breathing through your nose controls your heartbeat. That is what gives you endurance. You take so much oxygen into the lungs and the lungs control the heartbeat. Also, in the ring you have to wear a mouthpiece and then you can only breathe through your nose.

WHAT ARE BREATHING PATTERNS?

Your breathing pattern is the manner in which you take in and release oxygen. It is always done through the nose. The basic breathing pattern is a double short breath in and one breath out. Each individual will develop his own breathing pattern from the basic one. For example, my breathing pattern is one breath in and a double short breath out, just the opposite from the basic.

WHAT ARE THE BEST HOURS TO RUN?

The best hour to run is between 5:00 am and 6:00 am. In the morning your stomach is empty, you think your sharpest and you will be able to run your hardest. Also, the air is the cleanest it will be all day.

The next best time to run is between 10:00 pm and 11:00 pm. In the evening you may not be able to push your hardest because you still have food in your stomach, but at least the air will be clean.

WHAT IS A GOOD RULE OF THUMB ON THE DISTANCE TO RUN?

It all depends. I say for each round a person fights, he should run one mile. Six miles should be the limit whether a person is an amateur (three rounds) or a professional (four rounds and up). That is a good rule of thumb. It's not how far you run, it's *how* you run that makes the difference.

WHY IS SPRINTING IMPORTANT?

Sprinting is important for tearing tissues in the lungs so they can expand. You learn to take sprints at a time and control your heartbeat. Your breathing pattern in running is the same as fighting in the ring. Your sprints are the same as your actual fighting or attacking. Your walking is your footwork after you've attacked.

WHAT IS THE BENEFIT OF HILL RUNNING OR BLEACHER RUNNING?

In hill running you stride forward. It is more for building up the legs than for real endurance. In bleacher running, you always stay on the balls of your feet. This too is more for building the legs than for the kind of endurance a distance run can give you.

WHAT IS THE BEST SURFACE TO RUN ON?

It is best to run on either grass or dirt. You don't want to run on pavement if you can help it. The impact on the pavement is too hard for ankles and knees and you might develop shin splints.

HOW DO YOU PREVENT FOOT INJURIES WHILE RUNNING?

You have to wear good running shoes and find a good surface to run on. Know your limit in running. If you have weak ankles or knees make certain that they are properly supported.

ARE THERE WAYS OF PREVENTING SIDE ACHES WHILE RUNNING?

Yes, there are. First, make certain your stomach is empty. Next, be conscious of how you run. Make certain that you run with your spine straight and in an upright position, and don't shift your body from side to side.

IS RUNNING WITH ANKLE WEIGHTS BENEFICIAL?

The only place you should have weights when you run is around your waist. This way it keeps your weight centered. If you keep weights on your legs, they will tire out too quickly. When your legs get tired with weights there is more of a chance of injury.

WHICH IS BEST TO BUILD ENDURANCE, CLIMBING OR RUNNING?

There is no activity that can be mentioned that is better than running to build endurance. I am not talking about muscle endurance, I am talking about the endurance that controls the heartbeat. We work on muscle endurance in another section of this book.

IS THE SPEED BAG GOOD FOR CONDITIONING?

Yes, but for conditioning your eyes and hands only. It's used more for coordination.

WHAT IS A TIMING BAG?

It is a bag which develops your eye gap and hands. Since the bag moves in so many different directions, you need to develop good eye distance in order to get the timing to hit it.

HOW GOOD IS A MEDICINE BALL IN TRAINING?

It's very good. You have to practice throwing a medicine ball with your wrist and your arms. It is good for learning how to take impact at the time it hits. You have to be able to tighten your gut at the moment of impact and give a kiai.

IN GETTING INTO SHAPE SHOULD YOU BEGIN WITH STRETCHING OR ENDURANCE EXERCISES?

You've got to stretch. You have to be limber in order to develop endurance.

SHOULD YOU EXERCISE AFTER RUNNING OR BEFORE?

Both. You exercise before so that you don't pull any muscles. When your muscles are hot after running, you will be able to stretch a little further than when you first began running. It will also cool down your muscles without cramping.

WHAT IS THE QUICKEST WAY TO WARM UP?

It all depends on the type of workout you will be doing after the warm-up. We cover different types in the book, but for a general quick warm-up, jumping jacks and/or skipping rope are good.

WHAT IS THE ADVANTAGE OF EXERCISING WITH A PARTNER?

Mentally, a partner gives you competition. He will give you the incentive to push a little harder. You can do more advanced exercises if you have a partner. Also, it is more fun if you have someone there going through the grind with you.

ARE BOXERS IN BETTER CONDITION THAN KARATE FIGHTERS?

Yes they are, because they are always getting hit, and they have to be in very good condition. They are always working on power, speed and impact. Their bodies are conditioned to take that impact. In the martial arts, most competitors don't get hit with that kind of impact often enough to be conditioned for it.

In traditional tournaments, a person might get hit during thirty seconds out of a three-minute time period, and even then the hits are controlled. In boxing, the fighter is getting hit constantly during the round, so he has to be in better shape.

WHAT IS THE PROPER AMOUNT OF TIME ONE SHOULD WORK OUT EVERY DAY?

Ideally, for professionals, one should work out a good four hours, but not all at once. It should be spread out. You run for an hour in the morning. In the afternoon, have a two-hour work-out which is more physical. In the evening, do an hour or so of exercise work-out. That way working out becomes natural because it is being done all the time throughout the day. The nonprofessional might want to work out from two to three hours per day as his schedule permits.

HOW GOOD ARE DYNAMIC TENSION OR ISOMETRIC EXERCISES?

These exercises are a way of giving you inner strength. They are very good. I believe in inner strength.

ARE THERE WAYS OF STRENGTHENING THE ORGANS SO THEY CAN TAKE IMPACT?

No, but there are certain muscles around the organs you can strengthen. Joints can never be strengthened to take impact.

SPRINTING

1. Take the starting position.

2. Lift your knees high, tuck the body in, keep the chest forward. Remember to pump the arms continuously.

3. Jogging is done with your spine straight, in a relaxed position. Always keep the body loose, and don't take big strides.

BASIC SIT-UPS

1. Lie flat on the floor, hands behind your head, feet straight out.

2. As you sit up, bring the left knee high to the chest.

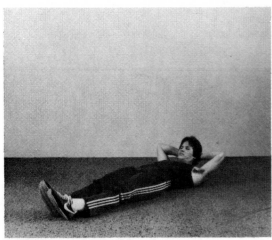

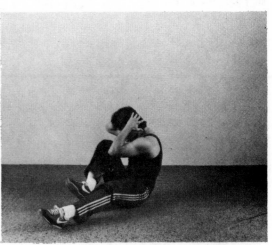

3. Return to the starting position.

4. As you sit up, bring the right knee high to the chest (minimum six reps).

INTERMEDIATE SIT-UPS (FOR LOWER STOMACH)

1. Lie flat on your back, hands behind your head, legs at a 90 degree angle.

2. Lift your head and touch your knees 25 times.

Remember: Breathe out when going up; breathe in when going down.

INTERMEDIATE SIT-UPS (FOR UPPER STOMACH)

1. Lie flat on your back, hands behind your head. Cross your ankles and bend your knees.

2. Bring your knees and chest together, minimum 20 reps.

Note:
For a routine: 25 reps for the lower stomach
20 reps for the upper stomach
15 reps for the lower stomach
10 reps for the upper stomach
5 reps for the lower stomach

ADVANCED SIT-UPS #1

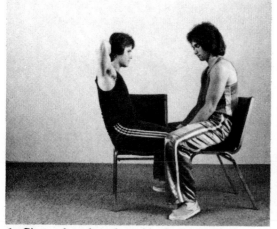

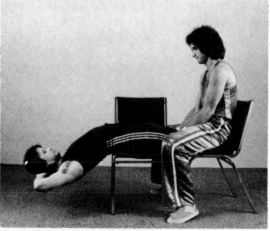

1. Sit on the edge of a table, bench or chair with hands behind your head. Legs are straight, with someone holding them for support.

2. Begin lowering your upper torso, moving past the horizontal position and continuing as far as you can go.

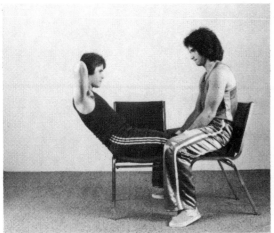

3. Lift up to the starting position and do 10 reps.

4. Now do a series of small sit-ups, never going below the horizontal position—10 reps.

Note: Advanced students should do 30 reps.

ADVANCED SIT-UPS #2

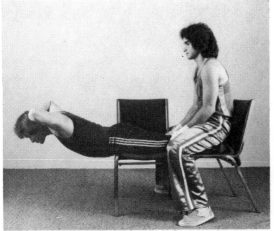

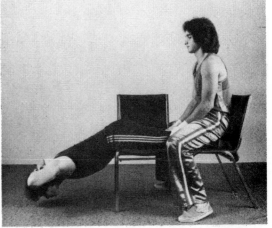

1. Lie on your stomach with your upper body hanging over a table, bench or chair. Your hands are behind your head.

2. Lower your body until you almost touch the floor.

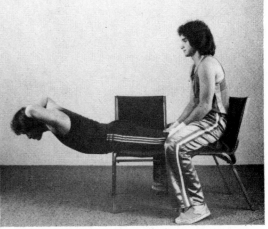

3. Raise your body past the horizontal position, 15 reps.

4. Keep your body parallel to the floor and pump, 15 reps.

LEG-UPS

1. Stand in a horse stance.

2. Squat, with 90 percent of your weight on your left foot.

3. Push off on the left leg and twist your torso to the left side.

4. Squat back down to the left side.

5. Transfer 90 percent of your weight to your right side in a squat position.

6. Push off with the right leg and twist your torso to the right side.

7. Squat down on the right side. Repeat.

LEG STRETCH FOR GROIN AND INSIDE THIGH

1. Spread your legs as wide as you can, hands on the floor in front of you.

2. The left hand grabs the left ankle. Put your right hand underneath the left thigh.

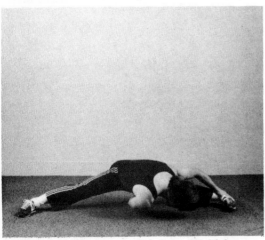

3. Push your head to the left knee. Hold for ten seconds.

4. Return your hands to the floor in front of you.

Leg Stretch for Groin and Inside Thigh

5. Grab the right ankle with the right hand. Keep your torso parallel to the floor while supporting your weight with the left hand.

6. Lift your torso slightly.

7. The left hand grabs your right thigh. Push your head to the right knee and hold for ten seconds.

8. Return to starting position.

SIDE STRADDLES FOR CALF AND THIGH

1. Get in a squat position with 90 percent of your weight on the left foot, toes pointed forward.

2. Your right hand grabs the left ankle. Your head is by the knee. Lock the right knee. Keeping your head on the knee, straighten the left leg and hold for 30 seconds.

3. Return to starting position.

4. Staying in the same position, switch your weight to the right leg.

5. The left hand grabs the right ankle. With your head on the knee, lock your left knee.

6. Return to the starting position.

LEG STRETCH: BACK OF LEGS AND LOWER BACK

1. Start in the squat position, on the balls of the feet, fingers touching the ground.

2. Place your palms flat on the floor, fingers facing each other, and lock your knees. Hold for 30 seconds.

3. Return to the original position.

4. Cross the right ankle over the left.

5. Lock legs and hold for 30 seconds.

6. Squat down.

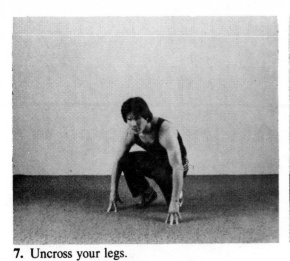

7. Uncross your legs.

8. Cross the left leg over the right.

9. Lock your legs, keeping palms on the ground, fingers facing each other. Hold for 30 seconds.

10. Return to the squat position.

FORWARD STRETCHING

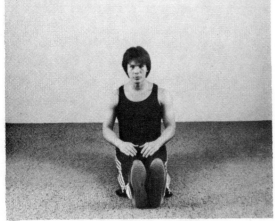

1. Sit flat on the floor, hands in front, palms facing inward.

2. Lean forward, finger tips touching in front of the shoes, palms facing outward. Hold for 30 seconds and return to the start.

SIDE STRADDLES

1. Start in the squat position with your weight on the left side, hands together, arms parallel to the floor, and right leg straight.

2. Push off with the left leg to a locked position, while twisting the upper torso to the left side.

3. Keeping the body in the same position, twist your upper torso to the right side. This time spread your arms.

4. Keeping the body in the same position, twist your torso to the left. Your arms remain spread.

5. Return to the starting position, your weight on the left side.

6. Transfer your weight to the right side, left leg straight, hands together.

7. Push off with the right leg to a locked position, twisting the upper torso to the right side.

8. Keeping your body in the same position, twist your upper torso to the left side. This time spread your arms.

9. Keeping your body in the same position, twist your torso to the right. Arms remain spread.

10. Return to the starting position, your weight on the right side.

STRADDLE SPLITS

1. Sit on the floor with your back straight and legs spread.

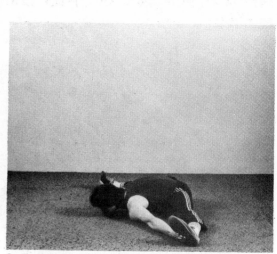

2. Roll forward, spreading your legs to their maximum extension and touching your chin to the ground.

3. Put your hands way back and lean back as well.

4. Start to pull your body backwards, letting your legs close naturally, without any help on your part.

5. This is the way to safely close your legs without risking a muscle pull or tear from a spread position.

PUSH-UPS FOR BACK OF ARMS, SHOULDERS AND SHOULDER BLADES

1. Begin in the push-up position.

2. Go down halfway.

3. Pump, only rising halfway up.

4. Do a minimum of 25 reps.
   Note: Keep your hands shoulder width apart, head looking up. Breathe out as you go down and inhale as you rise up.

ELEVATED PUSH-UPS

1. Get in push-up position, feet elevated higher than your shoulders.

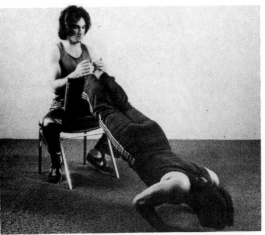

2. Do at least 10 push-ups, up to 40 if you're in good shape.

ENDURANCE PUSH-UPS

1. Begin in a standing position.

2. Get in the push-up position.

3. From the push-up position, begin the motion up . . .

4. Down . . .

5. And up. Pull the right knee up and stand up.

6. Turn around.

7. Get in the push-up position.

8. From the push-up position, begin the upwards motion again.
Note: Every time you turn around, add one extra push-up until you reach 10, then continue by decreasing one every time you turn.

PUSH-UPS FOR CHEST

1. Take the push-up position, with hands approximately three feet apart.

2. Lower down, then up.
Note: Do a minimum of 10 reps, 25 if you're in good condition. Keep your head down. Do the push-ups slowly, exhaling when going down and inhaling when rising up.

STOMACH TENSOR #1

1. Sit on the floor, feet six inches off the ground, arms parallel and straight out to the side.

2. Begin to rotate your arms in a circular motion, bringing them first to the front.

3. Once they reach the front, begin to return the arms to the starting position by rotating them.

4. End in the starting position, 10 reps.

WAIST TRIMMER #1

1. Sit on the floor, feet spread, hands behind your head, elbows out.

2. With your left elbow try to touch your left ankle by leaning forward.

3. Sit up straight again.

4. Lean toward your right ankle, trying to touch it with your elbow.

NECK EXERCISES FOR IMPACT

1. Your partner lies on his stomach, forearms to his side. Stand over your partner with your hands on his head.

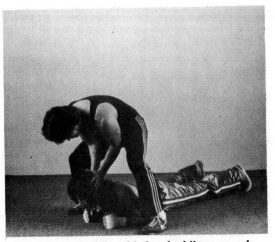

2. Your partner raises his head while you push on it.

STOMACH TENSOR #2

1. Sit on the floor with your legs six inches off the ground, your hands under your chin.

2. Begin to flutter kick, beginning with the right leg . . .

3. And then with the left leg.

4. After completing that series, put your legs together as in your starting position.

5. Spread your legs as wide as you can.

6. Then cross your right leg over your left.

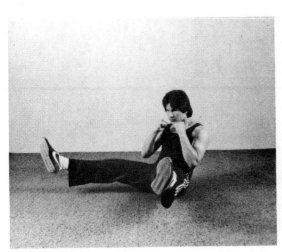

7. Open your legs.

8. Then cross your left leg over your right.

9. While still in the same position, pull your left knee to your chest . . .

10. Then pull your right knee to your chest. These exercises should be done with rhythm and a beat.

1. Sit on the floor, legs spread, hands behind your head. Twist your torso to the left side, touching your nose to your knee.

2. Twist to the right side, touching your nose to your knee.

3. Push forward to your left side, extending your hands beyond the foot.

4. Push forward to your right side, extending your hands beyond the foot.

ANKLE STRETCHES

1. Sit with your knees bent outward, the soles of your feet touching, rear and heels close together.

2. Lean forward, putting your weight on the ankles.

3. Bounce gently.

4. Return to the starting position.

DYNAMIC TENSION

1. Sitting on the ground, face your partner, legs spread. Grab your partner's wrists and pull while he resists without fighting.

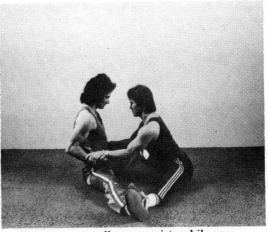

2. Your partner pulls your wrists while you resist.

1. Partners face one another, legs spread. Put your feet on the inside of your partner's ankles.

2. Push your partner's torso to the right side of his body.

3. Push your partner's torso to the left side of his body.

4. Sit up straight and grab your partner's wrists.

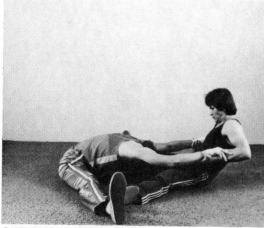

5. Pull your partner forward.

1. Stand in back of your partner, hands on his shoulders.

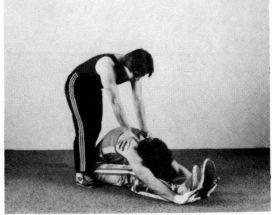

2. Push his torso down.

3. Straddle his back while pushing on his shoulders.

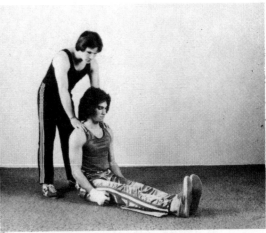

4. Return to the starting position.

5. Sit in front of your partner, your knees against his ankles.

6. Pull him toward you so his heels are close to his rear.

7. With your hands placed on his knees, push down gently.

8. Pull the knees up and begin to push down again, gently bouncing them.

FLEX, INTERMEDIATE FOR TWO PEOPLE #3

1. Your partner sits on the floor, legs spread, while you hold the wrists of his locked arms.

2. Place your foot between your partner's shoulder blades.

3. Slowly push your partner down, trying to touch his chin to the floor.

4. Slowly lift his body to an upright position.

FLEX, INTERMEDIATE FOR TWO PEOPLE #4

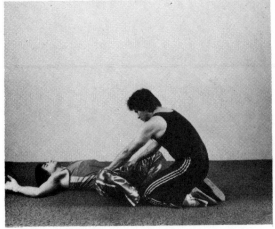

1. Your partner lies flat on his back, legs bent, while you pull him in to close the distance between his heels and rear.

2. Lace fingers with your partner.

3. Step on your partner's left knee . . .

4. Then on his right knee . . .

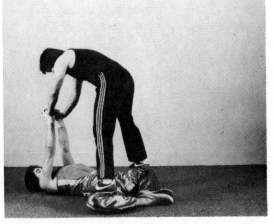

5. Then lean forward and push back your partner's hands.

6. Return to an upright position.

FLEX, INTERMEDIATE FOR TWO PEOPLE #5

 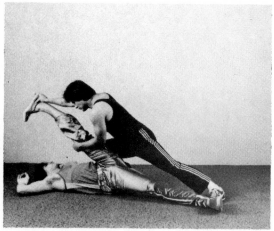

1. Your partner lies flat on his back. His leg is 90 degrees to the floor. Put your leg against his upright leg while holding on to the foot.

2. Use one hand to pull on the knee. The other hand pushes on the ankle. This will gently stretch the leg.

FLEX, INTERMEDIATE FOR TWO PEOPLE #6

1. Your partner lies on his side. His leg is 90 degrees to the floor. Put your leg next to his upright leg for support while grasping the foot with both hands.

2. Gently push your partner's leg up.

FLEX, INTERMEDIATE FOR TWO PEOPLE #7

1. Your partner lies flat on his back with his foot resting on your stomach.

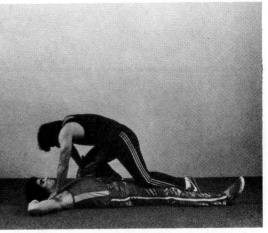

2. Lean forward, pushing your partner's leg gently back.

ENDURANCE ROUTINES   Jumping With Partner

1. Your partner starts on his hands and knees.

2. Jump over your partner sideways.

3. When you land, jump again.

1. Step on your left foot with your right foot behind you.

2. Switch to your right foot with your left foot behind you.

Duck Walk

1. Squat with your hands on your lapels.

2. Walk in this position for 200 feet.

Skipping Rope

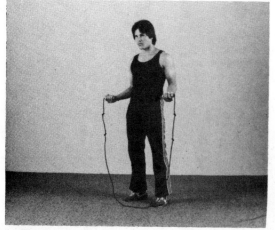

1. Start in a relaxed standing position.

2. Jump with rhythm for 10 to 20 minutes.

Bunny Hop

1. Squat with your hands behind your head.

2. Hop for 200 feet.

NECK BRIDGE

1. Lie on your back, feet flat on the floor, hands on your lapels.

2. Rise onto the top of your head, rocking back and forth slightly.

3. Turn your body from the outside . . .

4. To the inside. Grasp your thighs . . .

Neck Bridge

5. Rock back and forth slightly . . .

6. And bring your legs close to your body.

7. Flip over to the outside.

8. Rise onto the top of your head and repeat.

JAW BREAKER

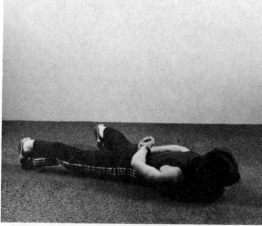

1. Place your chin on a pad, legs shoulder width apart, and hands behind your back.

2. Raise your rear end high. Your body is completely off the ground. The only points of contact should be your chin and the toes of your feet.

DYNAMIC PUSH-UPS, FOR SHOULDERS, FOREARMS, LOWER BACK AND CALVES

1. Start with legs spread, shoulder width apart, palms in front, thumbs touching.

2. Push up and hold for five seconds. Do a minimum of six reps.

HANDSTAND PUSH-UPS

1. Get in the handstand position, leaning your feet against the wall for support. Hands should be shoulder width apart.

2. Lower your body. Do not let your head touch the ground. Do a minimum of five reps.

IMPACT

Out of all of the questions regarding competition, no area has more of an air of mystery surrounding it than the issue of impact—how to take it, more than how to give it. There are many ways of handing out punishment to your opponent and only two ways of taking it, badly or like a pro.

Let's face it, nobody likes to get hit, so most of us avoid it. I try to avoid it like anybody else, but I can't ignore the inevitable, especially in my line of work.

The only true way of knowing if your technique creates pain is to have it performed on yourself. I don't mean absorbing the full impact, but rather taking a portion of that impact so you can imagine what a full force technique would feel like to your opponent. Obviously you don't have to get kicked in the groin or thumbed in the eye (if they were legal techniques) to know what the pain would feel like.

In learning to accept impact, note that there are three types that can occur in a fight. A stinging or slapping impact occurs when a technique is snapped or controlled. You experience this type of impact in traditional tournaments where a move is pulled short of maximum effect.

The other types of impact that you will experience in the ring are a shattering impact and a breaking impact. A shattering impact shocks the body, but it doesn't move the body from its planted position. The technique is snapped similar to the way a stinging impact is snapped. A breaking impact utilizes a follow-through technique. That kind of impact will move the body either backwards or to the side, depending on what you want. You might, for example, deliver a combination of a shattering impact technique and a breaking impact techinque. One is to shock your opponent's body without moving him and the other is to finish him off with a breaking impact.

To get into a fight and to receive an impact that your body has never felt before sends a shock throughout your system and the body tells the brain to give up, to stop this punishment. If, on the other hand, the body is used to taking the impacts, then it is really no big deal to get hit. Your body is accustomed to it. You know what it feels like so it is no surprise. You know the pain your opponent is experiencing, so you know what damage your technique can do.

There are certain parts of the body that cannot be conditioned to take impact. These are the joints, the groin, the face (which includes the nose), and the organs, so don't even try to get them used to taking impact. The muscles around your organs, and the muscle that covers your body, legs and arms are what we will be working on.

When people see me fight, they don't think I feel any pain. That is not so. I feel pain just like anybody else. The only difference is that I have conditioned my body to the pain so it is not a shock to my system when I get hit. I do feel the pain, but you will never see it register on my face or in my moves. The whole idea is to never let your opponent know that you do hurt.

The way you train is the way you react. I never wear any kind of shin pads, arm pads or protective equipment of any kind, save for a cup and a mouthpiece, when I train. I want to experience as much as possible while training so there will be no surprises waiting for me in the ring.

The following is a series of impact training techniques that can be done alone or with a partner.

It is important for you to start off these exercises gently and work your way up gradually in intensity. In a short amount of time your body will accept this pain and it will be no big deal for you either.

None of the impact practice techniques are aimed at a joint, groin, throat, spine, instep or neck. Be certain, as a partner, you watch very closely the areas with which you work. They are clearly shown in the following photographs.

Remember, whether you are a tournament competitor or a professional fighter, the reality of a fight in the street never ends when one person hits the ground. It ends when one person can't continue. So these exercises are good for everyone to experience. Knowledge is power and once you know and understand these concepts there is never a need to fear them again.

STINGING IMPACT TO THE BODY AND LEGS

1. Stand with legs shoulder width apart to the side, arms at your side, bent at a 90 degree angle above the head.

2. Your partner delivers a slap to the midsection.

3. He delivers a slap to the back of the legs.

4. He slaps the shin.

5. He slaps the side.

6. He slaps the calf.

7. He slaps the top of the thigh.

8. He slaps the back. He slaps every part of the body except below the ankles and above the neck.

FOREARM IMPACT (TO OUTSIDE OF ARM)

1. Each partner puts his left arm out until it meets the other's forearm.

3. Strike . . .

5. Strike . . .

2. Each partner then puts his right fist behind his left ear.

4. Raise the arm . . .

6. Raise the arm (and strike.) Continue to work the routine.

FOREARM IMPACT (TO INSIDE OF ARM)

1. Each partner raises his right arm behind his head as shown . . .

2. And strikes his partner's forearm.

3. Each partner raises his left arm behind his head . . .

4. And strikes the other's forearm.

BREAKING IMPACT ON TOP OF THIGHS

1. Raise your fists over your head.

2. Work up to full impact on top of thighs.

BREAKING IMPACT ON BACK OF THIGHS

1. Raise your fists over your head.

2. Swing them in back of you until they are parallel to the floor.

3. Hit the back of your thighs with the tops of your fists.

4. Swing back again and repeat.

BREAKING IMPACT ON LIVER

1. Put your left hand over the right, hands above head.

2. Work up to full power impact.

BREAKING IMPACT TO GUT WITH PARTNER

1. Face your partner. Thrust your left fist into his gut while he thrusts his left fist into yours.

2. Switch.

3. Impact.

4. Switch and impact.

BREAKING IMPACT ON GUT AND BLADDER

1. Put your left hand over the right, hands above head.

2. Work up to full power impact.

BREAKING IMPACT INSIDE THIGHS WITH PARTNER

1. Stand in a horse stance, with arms at your side in a 90 degree angle to the floor. Your partner stands in back of you and kicks your left thigh with his right leg, making impact with his instep.

2. He plants his foot.

3. Then he kicks the right thigh with his left instep.

4. He plants his foot and kicks your left thigh with his right instep. Your partner must be certain to look at the target, and not kick the back of the knee.

BALANCE

CAN ONE LEARN TO DEVELOP GOOD BALANCE?

Yes, through practice. First you learn to walk properly. Then you learn to balance yourself on one foot. Then you learn to balance yourself while in the air.

WHAT IS THE PROPER METHOD OF BALANCING YOURSELF?

Keep your feet shoulder width apart so that your body is centered in itself. This holds true if you are walking forward or backward. Your weight should always be centered in yourself. In a fighting position, your feet should be a little wider than shoulder width apart.

WHY IS BALANCE IMPORTANT?

In order to use your weapons in an effective manner you have to have good balance. If you're striking an opponent and your balance is off, half of your power is gone and you're prevented from using a follow-through. When you strike, providing you are well balanced, all of your power is equalized.

CAN YOU MAINTAIN AS MUCH BALANCE IN THE AIR AS YOU CAN ON THE GROUND?

Yes, although it requires more skill. Most people are afraid of using weapons in the air, but done properly you can balance as good in the air as you can on the ground. A technique done in the air has more impact because all of your weight as well as your power is coming into your opponent.

SHOULD ONE FIGHT FROM A WIDE OR A NARROW STANCE?

Always fight from a narrow stance. If you are too wide you have to make two steps in your move. You have to throw your weight up in order to move your leg. The result is a slow technique which is telegraphed to your opponent.

DOES AN ABILITY TO BALANCE ON ONE LEG GIVE YOU OVERALL BETTER BALANCE?

Not really. Balancing on one leg is good for kicks, but there is a different type of balance for two feet.

IS PRACTICING BALANCE BLINDFOLDED A GOOD METHOD?

Yes, it is. Now you are using your feet to balance instead of your eyes.

ARE THERE ANY MARTIAL ARTS WHICH EMPHASIZE BALANCE MORE THAN OTHERS?

Korean styles use many kicking techniques and that requires good balance for many of their moves. The soft style of kung-fu also requires a lot of balance.

WHAT DOES "LEARNING HOW TO WALK" MEAN?

That exercise shows you how to keep your weight centered in yourself in a forward motion. It means always being in balance.

WALKING WITH A NATURAL BALANCE

1. Start with your face forward, and feet shoulder width apart. Walk, keeping your feet shoulder width apart at all times.

2. Stop, bend your knees, and turn on the balls of your feet until the toes are facing 1:00.

ONE LEG TOE TOUCH

1. Stand with one knee cocked.

2. Shift your torso forward.

3. Touch your toes with one hand.

4. Return to the starting position.

TOE-HEEL WALKING

1. Start in a fighting position, with feet shoulder width apart.

2. Take a step with the forward leg.

3. Drag the back leg.

4. Step with the forward leg.

5. Drag the back leg.
   Step-drag, step-drag with rhythm.

6. With the forward leg as the base, pivot the back leg to a 90 degree angle, thus changing directions. Begin the routine over again. Do this with rhythm and a beat.

BALANCE-BODY WEAVING

1. Stand straight, feet together, elbows bent, hands under your chin.

2. Turn to a 90 degree angle.

3. Bend your torso to the left side, parallel to the floor.

4. Rotate to the front.

5. Continue your rotation to the right side.

6. Straighten your torso while keeping your body in the twisted position.

ONE LEG BALANCE

1. Stand on one leg, knees bent, arms straight out to the side.

2. Tilt your body to the left side as far as you can.

3. Tilt your body to the right side as far as you can.

4. Return to the starting position.

SHIFTING ONE LEG BALANCE

1. Raise one leg slightly off the floor in front of you, pointing the toes. Hold your arms straight out to your side.

2. Moving your arm in an arc, slowly bring it to the side of your body.

3. Continue the arc to the back.

4. Having reached the back position, pull your torso parallel to the floor.

ONE LEG HOP

1. Stand on one leg, with a towel next to your foot.

2. Jump in the air.

3. Land on the other side of the towel. Continue the same routine by jumping backwards and forwards.

ONE LEG KICKING ROUTINE   A. FRONT KICK

1. Stand up with knees bent.

2. Lift up your knee.

3. Slowly kick it out.

4. Return the knee to a cocked position.

B. SIDE KICK

1. Cock your knee to the side.

2. Extend your leg slowly and then return to the starting position.

C. BACK KICK

1. Lift your knee high.

2. Push your torso forward as you slowly kick your leg back.

3. Slowly bring your leg back.

4. Return the leg to the cocked position.

SQUAT ROTATIONS

1. Start in a semi-squat position looking over the left shoulder.

2. Extend your right leg, moving it in an arc.

Squat Rotations

3. Continue that arc with the right leg as far as possible.

4. Shift your weight to the right leg and continue the arc with the left leg extended.

5. Continue moving the left leg until it reaches a point where you must shift your weight again.

6. Shift your legs and continue the arc. Note: The forward motion is in 360 degree full circle turns.

ONE LEG COMBAT DRILLS

1. Face your partner while both of you are on one foot, hands in a fighting position.

2. Begin to slowly throw punches at your partner.

3. You block . . .

4. And counter.

JUMPING BODY ROTATION

1. Assume a forward stance. Your weight is evenly distributed with your left foot forward.

2. Jump in the air and spin 360 degrees.

3. Land with perfect balance.
Repeat the exercise by jumping in the opposite direction.

EVADING AND BLOCKING

WHAT DOES EVADING ENTAIL?

Evading means redirecting your opponent's weapons without having to make contact. This is done by moving out of the way without getting hit.

WHAT IS BOBBING AND WEAVING?

Bobbing is dodging with your head as your opponent's weapon comes toward you. Weaving is done with the upper part of your body.

WHAT IS A PARRY?

A parry is a defense in which you redirect your opponent past his target area.

WHAT IS THE DIFFERENCE BETWEEN FEINTING AND FAKING?

A feint is a hesitational movement you do with your head. You test your opponent by getting his reaction to your movement. Faking means you appear to use one weapon but then stop that action to use another. You feint with the head and fake with the body.

WHAT IS REDIRECTING?

Redirecting is moving at an angle away from your opponent's weapons, but toward his body. You're the target area he is aiming for, but his target is no longer there. You have made him aim for a different area. For example, your opponent is punching you at twelve o'clock. You move in a "v" position to either eleven o'clock or one o'clock. You have now redirected his weapon.

WHAT IS THE BEST WAY TO DEVELOP THE SPEED NEEDED IN BOBBING AND WEAVING?

You learn to move on reflex by practicing repetition through sight and sound. You move on count. Don't take anything for granted. You practice by moving on command, not before and not after.

DO YOU HAVE TO BE EVASIVE BEFORE DELIVERING A TECHNIQUE?

Some styles believe in blocking and striking at the same time. I personally believe in striking without getting hit. The less you get hit the longer you will last. But you don't necessarily have to do that. You can just block and counter.

IN YOUR OPINION CAN A GOOD EVASIVE FIGHTER DEFEAT A GOOD OFFENSIVE FIGHTER?

Not really because one of his offensive techniques will sooner or later get you. You can't just be evasive without ever getting hit. A good offensive fighter knows that too. For that reason, I advocate offensive over defensive fighting.

ISN'T EVADING MORE WIDELY USED IN BOXING THAN IN KARATE?

Yes, it is. The reason for that is because boxers only have two weapons they have to worry about, their fists. They can get in there and strike. But because of the legs, contact karate fighting requires more distance.

WHY WOULD YOU JAM AN OPPONENT?

The object in jamming is to stop your opponent's weapons before he builds up momentum with an already executed technique.

IS JAMMING A GOOD DEVICE TO USE?

For some people it is. If you are a good close-in defensive fighter then it would be good to use. But if you are a better kicker and you don't know what to do with your opponent once you've jammed him, you might find yourself in trouble. If you are good at going in and out, then it is good to jam. Jamming and hand techniques go together, because you have nothing except your hands when you get in that close, unless you throw him.

IS IT TRUE THAT THERE IS NOT MUCH BLOCKING IN FULL-CONTACT COMPETITION?

A lot of people don't know how to block correctly. They would rather take the blow than to block. There are many techniques in blocking. From your waist up you block with your arms, from your waist down you block with your legs. Never reach for your opponent's weapons to block.

WHAT ARE SOME OF THE BLOCKING AREAS?

You can block with your shoulders, knees, thighs, arms, head, etc. There are many areas.

EVADING TO THE LEFT

1. Start in a fighting position with the left side forward.

2. Move the left foot forward to 11:00, left hand protecting the face.

3. Pull the right foot close to the left leg, keeping both knees bent. The right hand protects the groin.

4. Pivot and face your opponent with your right hand facing forward.

EVADING TO THE RIGHT

1. Start in a fighting stance.

2. Take a quarter step back with your left leg, raise your hand to cover your face.

3. Step to 2:00 with your right foot, drop the left hand to cover your groin.

4. Pull in your left knee and face the opponent.

EVADING BACK

1. Start in a fighting stance.

2. The rear leg moves slightly back, and your torso twists to the inside.

3. Drop into a squat position with the right hand covering the upper body (face), and the left hand covering the lower body (groin).

4. Return to the starting position.

BOBBING

1. Start in a fighting stance.

2. Move your head in a "V" position from the waist up. Your head goes to 11:00.

3. Move your head back to the original position.

4. Repeat, shifting your shoulders to the opposite side. Your head goes to 1:00.

WEAVING

1. Start in a fighting stance.

2. Drop your body and begin to move your back shoulder forward.

3. Continue until your back shoulder is now forward. This motion is done in a "U."

4. Your head goes to 1:00.
Remember: This is a quick motion. You are evading a hand technique and are setting yourself up to counter.

FEINTING DOWN

1. Start in a fighting stance.

2. Drop your knees quickly, keeping your body straight.

FEINTING BACK

1. Start in a fighting stance.

2. Move your body back, putting weight on the rear foot, and move your head back at the same time.

Remember: These feinting exercises are done with quick short movements.

ROLLING WITH THE PUNCH

1. Start in a fighting stance.

2. Begin turning your head without moving your feet.

3. Continue turning your head from the impact.

4. Return to the starting position.

This exercise helps you avoid taking the full impact of a punch. Your neck must be strong but loose.

REDIRECTING WITH THE REAR PALM

1. Start in a fighting stance.

2. Your opponent attacks your head with his left hand.

3. Redirect his punch to your left by using your right hand.

4. Wind up and be ready to counter.

SHOULDER ROLL

1. Start in a fighting stance.

2. Your opponent attacks the upper body.

3. Begin twisting your front shoulder, causing the blow to glance off.

4. Counter the attack.

REDIRECTING WITH THE FOREARM

1. Start in a fighting stance.

2. Your opponent attacks with a punch to the body.

3. Pivot your body sharply to your right side.

4. Follow through with a counter punch.

BRIDGING THE GAP

1. Start in a fighting stance.

2. Move forward, slightly advancing the lead foot and dragging the back foot forwards.

3. Then shift your weight back, keeping your feet stationary.

4. Continue moving slightly forward with each repetition.

CLINCHING

1. Start in a fighting stance.

2. When your opponent throws a left jab, bob to your left.

3. Pivot, wrapping your left arm over and under his right forearm. Your right hand is on his left wrist.

4. Wrap your right arm over and under his right arm. Make certain that you lock both of his arms by holding them above his elbows. Tuck your head into his chest.

SMOTHERING BLOCK

1. Start in a fighting stance.

2. Your opponent jabs with his left.

3. You parry and smother his left hand to his chest with your hand.

4. Smother his right hand with your elbow.

LEG BLOCK

1. Start in a fighting stance.

2. Your opponent attacks with a right front kick. Thrust a palm over his eyes and block with your shin by raising your left knee.

3. Plant your foot back.

4. Counter with a roundhouse kick.

OUTSIDE LEG BLOCK

1. Start in a fighting stance.

2. When your opponent kicks with his left leg, block with your left shin.

3. Pivot and plant your foot.

4. Counter with a back kick with your right leg.

REAR LEG BLOCK

1. Start in a fighting stance.

2. Your opponent attacks with a round kick from the left side. Block it with your right shin.

3. Plant your foot back.

4. Deliver a roundhouse kick to the belt line.

DEFENSE AGAINST A REAR LEG KICK (HEEL THRUST)

1. Start in a fighting stance.

2. When your opponent starts to move, plant your foot back.

3. As the opponent kicks back with the rear leg, shift your body to the rear leg.

4. As he brings his foot back, jump towards him, cocking your left leg.

5. Deliver a side kick as his leg is pulled back in a cocked position.

DEFENSE AGAINST A JAB

1. Start in a fighting stance.

2. Your opponent attacks with a jab. Parry with your right hand.

3. Push your opponent's hand down.

4. Counter with a right cross.

DEFENSE AGAINST A RIGHT CROSS

1. Start in a fighting stance.

2. Your opponent comes in with a right cross.

Defense Against A Right Cross

3. Turn your body at a 90 degree angle to him and turn your face over your right shoulder (rolling your head with the punch). Jab with your left.

4. Face your opponent and cock your right arm.

5. Follow through with a right jab.

DEFENSE AGAINST A SPINNING BACK KNUCKLE

1. Your opponent spins in with a back knuckle.

2. You duck underneath his arm.

3. Rise on the other side of his arm.

4. Counter with a right hook to his liver.

5. Pull back.

6. Finish with a right hook to his jaw.

DEFENSE AGAINST A RIGHT UPPER CUT

1. Start in a fighting stance.

2. Your opponent begins to throw a right upper cut. Jam his fist with your right hand.

Defense Against A Right Upper Cut

3. Counter with a left upper cut.

4. Finish with a right hook.

DEFENSE AGAINST A FRONT KICK

1. Start in a fighting stance.

2. When your opponent cocks his knee, raise your knee slightly.

3. Jam his ankle.

4. Plant your foot forward, and move your left hand towards his lead shoulder.

5. Shoot an open palm thrust . . .

6. And a power shin kick.

DEFENSE AGAINST A ROUNDHOUSE KICK

1. Start in a fighting stance.

2. Your opponent begins to throw a roundhouse kick. Block with your shin by raising your knee up to a 90 degree angle. Thrust your left palm into his face for distraction.

3. Plant your foot back.

4. Deliver a roundhouse kick with the shin of that leg.

DEFENSE AGAINST A FORWARD LEG KICK

1. Start in a fighting stance.

2. Your opponent throws a kick with his forward leg while sliding up.

3. Jam his leg with your knee.

4. Plant your foot down lightly on its toe.

5. Raise your knee . . .

6. And deliver a side kick.

DEFENSE AGAINST A CROSSOVER ROUNDHOUSE KICK #1

1. Start in a fighting stance.

2. Your opponent begins a crossover . . .

3. And throws a roundhouse kick. Block with your shin and turn your body at a 45 degree angle.

4. Plant your foot back.

5. Deliver a roundhouse kick with the same leg.

DEFENSE AGAINST A FRONT BALL KICK

1. Start in a fighting stance.

2. As the opponent begins to deliver a kick, jam it with your shin.

3. Plant your foot down and spin on that foot.

4. Deliver a back kick with the opposite foot.

DEFENSE AGAINST A SPINNING BACK KICK #1

1. Start in a fighting stance.

2. Your opponent begins a spinning back kick.

3. As he kicks, take a deep step forward with the left foot.

4. Drag in the right foot. Put your right hand on his left shoulder.

5. Cock your left arm . . .

6. And shoot a left hook to his kidney.

DEFENSE AGAINST A SIDE KICK #1

1. Start in a fighting stance.

2. Your opponent skips in with a side kick, leg cocked.

Defense Against A Side Kick

3. Block his kick with your knee.

4. Plant your foot forward.

5. Follow through with a back sweep take down.

DEFENSE AGAINST A BACK ROUNDHOUSE KICK

1. Start in a fighting stance.

2. As the opponent shifts his weight to begin a kick, bob to the left.

3. Step out to the right as your opponent completes his kick.

4. Deliver a power kick to his calf.

DEFENSE AGAINST A CROSSOVER ROUNDHOUSE KICK #2

1. Start in a fighting stance.

2. As the opponent begins to cross over . . .

3. Bob to 11:00.

4. Deliver a power sweep to his calf.

1. Start in a fighting stance.

2. As the opponent begins to spin, plant your right foot back.

3. As he extends, you shift 90 percent of your weight to the back foot.

4. When his leg is brought back, transfer your weight.

5. Deliver a whip kick to his head.

DEFENSE AGAINST A SIDE KICK #2

1. Start in a fighting stance.

2. When your opponent begins to cross over, plant your foot back.

3. When he raises his leg and kicks, dip so his leg ends up behind your head.

4. Raise your knee . . .

5. And deliver a kick behind his knee.

YOU CAN 'T HIT WHAT'S NOT THERE!

(left to right) Gene LeBelle,Arnold Urquidez,Blinky Rodriguez,Rubin Urquidez,Benny,
Manuel Urquidez,Smiley Urquidez

HAND TECHNIQUES

ARE THE HAND TECHNIQUES DIFFERENT IN FULL-CONTACT KARATE THAN IN TRADITIONAL KARATE?

Yes. In full contact no down blows are allowed. Therefore, you can't use your chops or hammer blows. The basic hand weapons in full contact would be your jab, reverse knuckle punch, ridge hand and your spinning back knuckle. Mainly you'll work your hands as a boxer would.

DO YOU FEEL CIRCULAR HAND TECHNIQUES ARE BETTER THAN STRAIGHT ONES?

No. Straight hand techniques are the most effective. Going in a circular motion you hit to the outside of the body in a shattering impact. A straight technique would put you to the inside of the body with a breaking impact. It is faster because of the shorter distance and because you are throwing everything you have behind it.

DO BOXERS HAVE BETTER HANDS THAN KARATE FIGHTERS?

Yes, they do in the sport. In the street, of course, there are no rules. The reason boxers have better hands in the sport is because they know how to throw their weight behind their punches.

ARE HAND TECHNIQUES MORE IMPORTANT THAN FOOT TECHNIQUES?

From a close range, hand techniques work better. From a close range, you really have no choice but to use your hands. From a distance, your hands don't do you any good if your opponent is so far away that you either wouldn't be able to reach him or by reaching him you throw yourself off balance.

DO YOU FEEL THAT A STYLE THAT STRESSES BOTH HANDS AND FEET IN EACH TECHNIQUE IS THE BEST?

Yes. Any style that doesn't separate your weapons will be the most versatile.

IS SPEED OR POWER MORE IMPORTANT IN HAND TECHNIQUES?

Speed is always more important because you can pick away at your opponent. If you're always looking for that big one with power, the other fellow may already have you carved up.

IS IT TRUE THAT THE BIGGER YOUR ARMS THE HARDER YOUR PUNCH WILL BE?

Definitely. Larger arms carry a lot more weight, so naturally, they have a bigger impact. But also remember the bigger your arms get, the shorter your reach becomes.

HOW DO YOU FEEL ABOUT CALLOUSING YOUR HANDS TO GET POWER?

I don't agree with that. To put any kind of callouses on your hands affects you later on in life. All they are good for is show. You don't need to have callouses for power or strength. You don't need them to break bricks or boards. You do your breaking mentally, not physically.

ARE ELBOWS MORE POWERFUL THAN FISTS?

Yes. Elbows are your most powerful weapons from the waist up. The impact from an elbow is harder and faster than one from your fist because you are working on straight bone and you put your shoulder muscle behind it.

CAN ACUPUNCTURE HELP STRENGTHEN THE ARMS?

Yes. Acupuncture or acupressure can build speed and strength by working certain nerves. You can also deaden pain by working nerves. That can be helpful or harmful to you, depending on your reason and the circumstances behind your decision.

IS A BACK KNUCKLE AN EFFECTIVE WEAPON?

Not from a straight on position. It is more of a slapping impact. Now, if you spin around with that back knuckle technique, then you are using your weight and your momentum. That would make your contact a breaking or shattering impact. The only danger to a spinning back knuckle is if you miss your target. Then you would be spinning right into your opponent's weapons. There is always a danger with any spinning technique when you turn your back on an opponent.

HOW EFFECTIVE ARE RIDGE HAND TECHNIQUES?

They are good if you hit your target. They are not good for hitting the body or a big muscle. They're good for striking the temple, the jaw, the back of the ear, a pressure point, the neck or the bridge of the nose.

SHOULD YOU BLOCK AND STRIKE WITH THE SAME HAND?

You can, but it's better to block than to use the opposite hand to strike because then you are prepared to throw your body weight behind it.

ARE CHOPS ALLOWED IN FULL CONTACT KARATE?

No, they aren't. As a matter of fact, it is quite difficult to open your hand to a shuto or a chop when you have gloves on. Besides, down blows are not allowed in full contact.

WHAT IS MORE POWERFUL, A TRADITIONAL REVERSE PUNCH OR A RIGHT CROSS?

A right cross. A reverse punch uses the hip in a locking position which stops the action at the point of locking. With a right cross, you throw everything into it and there is no locking in the technique. Locking the hip is not a good idea when you're doing hand techniques. When you lock your hip it prevents you from throwing your opposite hand as quickly as you can by using a right cross. A right cross, being an unlocked technique, is more of a flowing motion.

HOW EFFECTIVE ARE JABS?

They are very effective in carving up your opponent by cutting him with the last second snap of the technique. You can weaken him with jabs.

WHAT ARE SOME OF YOUR HAND TECHNIQUES IN FULL CONTACT?

The main ones are your jabs, your right cross, left hook, upper cut, spinning back knuckle, winging right and ridge hands.

WHAT IS THE DIFFERENCE BETWEEN A POWER STRIKE AND A SNAPPING STRIKE?

A power strike is more of a breaking blow while a snapping strike is more of a shattering blow. If you want to set your opponent up for another technique, then you would use a shattering blow to shock his body. That gives you the opportunity to use another technique. A breaking blow is more of a follow-through in which you are pushing your opponent out of range of your hands. I usually use them both in combinations. I'll use a snapping strike to set him up for my power strike.

ARE PALM HEEL STRIKES MORE POWERFUL THAN FOREKNUCKLE PUNCHES?

A palm heel strike is more dangerous than a foreknuckle punch because you are using straight bone in a locking thrust position. You not only can use this as a thrust, but also in a shattering kind of impact as well.

FRONT JAB

1. Start in a fighting stance.

2. Your body is planted, and your left arm moves from the elbow.

Front Jab

3. Connect, and torque the fist at the last moment before impact.

4. Pull your hand back.

RIGHT CROSS

1. Start in a fighting stance.

2. Begin to drive your rear shoulder toward your opponent.

3. Snap your fist into the opponent.

4. Return to the starting position.

LEFT HOOK TO THE FACE

1. Start in a fighting stance.

2. Your right shoulder is driving toward your opponent, and your hips are turned counterclockwise. Your shoulders are facing the opponent at 3:00 and 9:00.

3. Your left hand begins to deliver the blow.

4. The hips twist with the punch. Then return to the starting position.

LEFT HOOK TO THE BODY

1. Start in a fighting stance.

2. Pivot your body and shoulder forward.

Left Hook to the Body

3. Begin driving your left fist into the body.

4. Complete the hook and return to the starting position.

UPPER CUT

1. Start in a fighting stance.

2. Dip your body by bending both knees.

3. Begin driving your rear shoulder and fist toward the opponent.

4. Make contact in an upward direction.

WINGING RIGHT TO THE BODY

1. Start in a fighting stance.

2. As you dip your body, your left shoulder comes forward.

3. Hips and shoulders twist forward.

4. Deliver the blow in a circular punch to the kidneys, knuckles facing in.

WINGING RIGHT TO THE FACE

1. Start in a fighting stance.

2. Dip your body with the left shoulder out.

Winging Right to the Face

3. Twist your hips and shoulder.

4. Deliver the blow in a circular punch.

SPINNING BACK KNUCKLE

1. Start in a fighting stance.

2. Dip your front shoulder.

3. Twist your body.

4. Deliver a back knuckle blow to the opponent's face.

WHIPPING ELBOW (ALLOWED IN THE ORIENT)

1. Start in a fighting stance.

2. Raise your right knee and lean toward your opponent.

3. Your elbow starts to rise.

4. Whip it around the opponent's eyebrow.

5. Follow through with a downward motion.

6. Step forward behind the opponent's leg as a set-up for a left cross.

TOP FIST STRIKE

1. Start in a fighting stance.

2. Wind up, bobbing to the left. Set up as you would for a left hook.

3. Throw your left shoulder forward, with elbow 95 percent extended. The top of the fist hits the temple.

4. Return to the starting position.

BOTTOM FIST STRIKE

1. Start in a fighting stance.

2. Bring your left shoulder back.

3. Bring your fist forward in an arc.

4. Follow through.

THRUST PALMING, TO THE HEAD

1. Start in a fighting stance.

2. Lean forward and raise your palm to the opponent's head.

3. Complete the strike, keeping your opponent at a distance.

THRUST PALMING, TO THE REAR SHOULDER

1. Start in a fighting stance.

2. Take a short step with the front foot and lean forward.

3. Open your fist and begin driving toward the opponent.

4. Strike the opponent hard on his rear shoulder.

FOREARM STRIKE, TO THE SHOULDER

1. Start in a fighting stance.

2. Slide up and smother your opponent's weapons.

3. Drive your front forearm forward into the opponent's shoulder.

DIRECT FOREARM STRIKE, TO THE FACE

1. Start in a fighting stance.

2. Lean forward and rotate your body. Dip by bending at the knees.

3. Step into the opponent while raising your body. Raise your forearm toward his face.

4. Drive your forearm into the jaw or chin of the opponent.

REVERSE FOREARM STRIKE, TO THE FACE

1. Start in a fighting stance.

2. Rotate your body, bringing your front hand back, palms facing out.

3. Step forward, rotate your body to the left and begin driving your forearm into the opponent. Snap at the last moment to strike him across the side of the face.

4. Rotate your body to the right, facing him squarely. You have now smothered his weapons, so he is set up for a finishing move.

JAB-RIGHT CROSS-LEFT HOOK

1. Start in a fighting stance.

2. Shoot a left jab to the opponent's jaw.

3. Use a right cross . . .

4. Then a left hook.

LEFT JAB-RIGHT HOOK-UPPER CUT

1. Start in a fighting stance.

3. A right hook . . .

2. Shoot a left jab . . .

4. And an upper cut.

JAB-LEFT BODY HOOK-LEFT HOOK TO HEAD

1. Start in a fighting stance.

2. Throw a left jab to the face.

3. Twist your body and throw the right shoulder forward.

4. Deliver a left body hook.

5. Twist the right shoulder forward.

6. End with a left hook to the jaw.

LEFT HOOK-RIGHT CROSS-LEFT HOOK

1. Start in a fighting stance.

2. As you move in on the opponent, throw your right shoulder forward.

3. Shoot a left hook to the jaw . . .

4. A right cross to the jaw . . .

5. And a left hook to the jaw.

6. Follow through.

LEFT JAB-RIGHT CROSS-LEFT CROSS

1. Start in a fighting stance.

2. Shoot a left jab to the face . . .

3. Then a right cross to the face . . .

4. And finally a left cross to the jaw.

JAB-SPINNING BACK KNUCKLE (RIGHT HAND)- SPINNING BACK KNUCKLE (LEFT HAND)

1. Start in a fighting stance.

2. Shoot a left jab to the face.

3. Begin to spin, cock your right arm, and look over your right shoulder.

4. With a closed fist, hit your opponent's right temple. Use the back of your hand.

5. Spin in the opposite direction, cocking your left hand and looking over your right shoulder.

6. With a closed fist, hit your opponent's left temple. Use the back of your hand.

RIGHT UPPER CUT-RIGHT HOOK-LEFT CROSS

1. Start in a fighting stance.

2. Dip your body by bending the legs.

3. Shoot a right upper cut under the heart, palm facing up.

4. Bring your right shoulder back.

5. Deliver a right hook to the face . . .

6. And a left cross to the jaw.

DIP-UPPER CUT-LEFT HOOK-RIGHT CROSS

1. Start in a fighting stance.

2. Dip your body by bending the legs.

3. Throw an upper cut under the chin, palm facing outward.

4. Deliver a left hook to the face, palm facing down, elbow bent at a 90 degree angle.

5. Bring your left shoulder back . . .

6. And finish with a right cross.

WINGING RIGHT TO THE BODY-WINGING RIGHT TO THE JAW-LEFT HOOK TO THE JAW

1. Start in a fighting stance.

2. Bring your right shoulder back and dip your body.

3. Shoot your right into the kidneys, palm facing out.

4. Pull back with your body and fist.

5. Shoot a right to the jaw . . .

6. And a left hook to the jaw.
Note: The arm is bent at a 90 degree angle. The power comes from the shoulder and the torque of the body.

LEFT JAB-BACK HAND-RIGHT CROSS

1. Start in a fighting stance.

2. Shoot a left jab to the face.

3. Strike to the side of the face, palm facing out.

4. Finish with a right cross to the face.

FOOT TECHNIQUES

HOW DO YOU DEVELOP POWER IN YOUR LEGS?

You can develop power by running and also by using weights. The main thing to do is to build up the endurance of your muscles. You gain endurance by running up bleachers and running up hills. The bigger your legs, the more power you will have behind them. In other words, the more weight you will have to throw. There are also power bags you can work out with. Any type of sport which involves short sprints where you have to move around quickly will also help you develop power. Anything which has to do with a squat or low position where your thighs are constantly being pushed can build power. Dynamic tension with a partner can also help you to develop power.

WHAT DO YOU THINK IS THE MOST POWERFUL KICK IN KARATE?

A spinning back kick is the most powerful, because you are spinning into your opponent in a locking thrust position and you are using bone to go straight through instead of a round type of a kick. I feel that the spinning back kick is one of the most powerful and dangerous kicks in the martial arts.

IS IT DANGEROUS TO USE JUMPING KICKS?

If you don't know how to use a jumping kick properly it can be dangerous. The dangerous part is coming down into your opponent's weapons if you've missed your target.

WHAT MUSCLES DO YOU HAVE TO STRETCH TO GET YOUR KICKS HIGH?

Mainly you work your groin, lower back, side of your hip and inner thigh muscles.

ARE LEGS OFTEN USED FOR BLOCKING?

Yes. As a matter of fact, in Japan and Thailand they block with their legs from the waist down. From the waist up they block with their hands. Remember, when you block you never want to reach for your opponent's weapons whether you're using your hands or your legs.

HOW DO YOU DEVELOP YOUR LEGS SO THEY DON'T FEEL THE PAIN FROM IMPACT?

You have to train your legs to take the blow and accept the pain without sending them into shock. The way fighters practice in Thailand is by kicking a banana tree with their shins. A banana tree is hard on the inside, but soft on the outside. The way we simulate this practice is by wrapping a carpet or rug around a pole. This will also prevent your skin from splitting.

The problem is that your legs are not ready to take the impact because they have never felt that kind of pain. When you shock your body by giving it an impact it has never felt, it retaliates right away. It wants to give up. You have to get used to it in practice by doing it constantly, slowly at first and then building up in intensity so it becomes something you can adjust to.

DO YOU PRACTICE SHADOW BOXING WITH YOUR LEGS?

Yes. I practice the same way that I shadow box with my hands, but I do it together in combinations.

IS IT GOOD TO USE HERBS FOR TOUGHENING YOUR SHINS?

I don't feel that using herbs to numb the legs is a good practice. You may hurt yourself or even break a leg and not even know it. By not knowing you have this injury you can further damage yourself, perhaps even for life, by continually using your legs after they have been hurt. The only time I believe in using herbs is to heal an injury.

ARE ANKLE WEIGHTS GOOD FOR PRACTICE?

No, ankle weights are bad. They throw your timing off, they throw your accuracy off and they get you tired quickly. When you take the weights off your speed will be quicker, but your accuracy will still be off because that is the way you have trained. If you want to use weights, put them around your waist so your weight is centered in yourself.

WHAT IS THE FASTEST WAY TO BUILD LEG MUSCLES?

Leg muscles can be built the fastest through running and dynamic tension.

HOW CAN I BUILD UP SPEED?

Build your speed by shadow boxing and kicking in the air. Kicking at some object in the air, such as a piece of paper, is excellent. Repetition builds up speed.

IS THERE ANY WAY A PERSON CAN PROTECT THEIR TOES WHILE KICKING?

Yes, by training your toes to go back. Always kick on the ball of your foot.

HOW DO YOU TRAIN TO DO JUMP KICKS?

You have to learn to go for height. Once you get height, you learn to jump forward at a 45 degree angle. When you get height, you learn how to spin. Then all of your kicks come into play.

WHAT IS THE DIFFERENCE BETWEEN THE KICKS IN TRADITIONAL KARATE AND FULL-CONTACT KARATE?

In traditional karate there is no follow through. You are trained to control your kicks. The kicks are always snapped. The way you train is the way you react. If you're always training to snap or control your technique, that will also be your reaction when you compete professionally or fight for real. In full contact, the technique is not controlled; it is followed through.

WHAT DIFFERENT TYPES OF KICKS ARE THERE IN FULL CONTACT?

In full contact there are really just two types of kicks. There are power kicks and whip kicks. There are no snap kicks. Power kicks are driven through your opponent at a 45 degree angle. Whip kicks are whipped around in a circular motion.

IN A REAL FIGHT IS IT BETTER TO KICK HIGH OR KICK LOW?

Actually it is better to kick low because you will have maximum speed and power. Also, the lower you are to the ground the better balance you have.

HOW DO YOU DEVELOP COORDINATION IN YOUR LEGS?

You can develop coordination by skipping rope, running, going through an obstacle course, by practicing katas and wazas, as well as by sparring.

SHOULD I WEAR SHIN GUARDS OR PADS WHILE TRAINING?

No. If you're going to train your body to accept the shock of impact you have to do it while you're training. You don't wear shin guards or pads in the ring so you shouldn't wear them while you train.

ARE KNEES ALLOWED IN FULL-CONTACT KARATE?

Kicks either with the knee or to the knee are not allowed in the United States rules for full contact. They are allowed, however, in Thailand and Japan.

POWER FRONT BALL KICK, WITH THE REAR LEG

1. Start in a fighting stance.

2. Bring your lead shoulder forward and pivot your hips. Bring your rear knee up inside of his elbow. The front knee is also slightly bent.

3. Drive forward and thrust your leg out to its full extension. Strike with the ball of your foot.

4. Snap your foot back and then plant your foot either forward or back.

POWER FRONT BALL KICK, WITH THE FORWARD LEG

1. Start in a fighting stance.

2. Thrust your left hand at the opponent's face. At the same time, switch feet without moving your shoulders.

3. Raise your left knee high. Keep your left hand in front of the opponent's face.

4. Thrust your kick forward into the opponent.

POWER ROUNDHOUSE KICK

1. Start in a fighting stance.

2. Rotate your hips and shoulders forward.

3. Switch feet and throw left jab.

4. Hop into the opponent, delivering a kick with your shin across his belt line.

SKIPPING KNIFE EDGE KICK

1. Start in a fighting stance.

2. Lean forward, thrusting your palm into the opponent's face.

3. Your shoulders are straight and your body weight is centered. Bring your knee up.

4. Skip into the opponent, thrusting your heel into his hip.

JUMPING SIDE THRUST KICK

1. Start in a fighting stance.

2. Your back shoulder and hip pivot forward.

3. Hop into the opponent.

4. Deliver a thrusting side kick.

HEEL THRUST KICK

1. Start in a fighting stance.

2. Pivot your hips and shoulders. Put your left palm into the opponent's face.

3. Cross behind with your rear leg.

4. Deliver the kick forward, driving through.

JUMP SPINNING BACK KICK (DEFENSIVE-GOING TO THE INSIDE)

1. Start in a fighting stance.

2. Dip your body low by bending at the knees.

3. Jump up while you pivot in the air.

4. Deliver the back kick.

SPINNING BACK KICK

1. Start in a fighting stance.

2. Throw your left palm into the opponent's face and drop your left hip.

3. Begin to pivot.

4. Bring your right foot past your left foot and lift.

5. Pivot and deliver a thrusting kick.

SPINNING WHEEL KICK

1. Start in a fighting stance.

2. Step forward, pivoting your shoulders and hips.

3. Pivot forward and dip low, knees bent, making the opponent concentrate down.

4. Lock your pivot leg and raise up, throwing the kick to your opponent's head with the leg fully extended.

JUMP SPINNING WHEEL KICK

1. Start in a fighting stance.

2. Step forward and dip.

3. Jump in the air and begin to pivot, extending your left leg.

4. Deliver the wheel kick while still in the air.

SWEEPING ROUNDHOUSE KICK

1. Start in a fighting stance.

2. Put your right hand in front of the opponent's face for distraction. Your body pivots forward.

3. Raise your knee.

4. Strike down hard below his calf.

JUMPING FORWARD SPINNING BACK KICK (OFFENSIVE-GOING TO THE OUTSIDE)

1. Start in a fighting stance.

2. Jump up and forward, bringing your rear leg to the front.

3. Begin to pivot in the air.

4. Complete the pivot in the air.

5. Deliver the back kick while still in the air.

THRUSTING HEEL KICK

1. Start in a fighting stance.

2. Slide your back foot up. Shoot your left palm into the opponent's face.

3. Raise your left knee, keeping your palm in the opponent's face.

4. Thrust your heel into the opponent's face.

JAMMING HEEL KICK (JOINT KICKING, ALLOWED IN THE ORIENT)

1. Start in a fighting stance.

2. Pivot your right shoulder forward.

3. Raise the back knee high.

4. Jam the opponent's knee with your heel. Twist your foot outward.

THIGH KICK

1. Start in a fighting stance.

2. Lean your body into your opponent, putting your left palm into his face so he cannot see.

3. Bend your knee.

4. Thrust the shin into your opponent's thigh.

DRAGON SWEEP

1. Start in a fighting stance.

2. Pivot your right shoulder forward.

3. Sweep the opponent's left leg off balance.

4. Drop on your right knee.

5. With both hands touching the ground for support, sweep your left leg around in an arc.

6. Catch the opponent's right leg with your sweeping leg.

LEAPING KNEE KICK (ALLOWED IN THE ORIENT)

1. Start in a fighting stance.

2. Pivot your body with the right side forward.

3. Step forward with your right foot and dip your body to your right.

4. Raise your left arm high as you leap off the ground.

5. Grab your opponent's head with your left hand.

6. Bring your left knee into the opponent's face as you push his face into it.

INSIDE SWEEPING KICK

1. Start in a fighting stance.

2. Slide your rear foot forward while putting your left palm into the opponent's face.

3. Raise your knee.

4. Kick the inside of your opponent's calf.

SCISSORS KICK (ALLOWED IN THE ORIENT)

1. Start in a fighting stance.

2. Pivot your body, bringing the rear shoulder forward.

3. Jump into your opponent, putting your right foot on your opponent's knee and hooking your left ankle in back of his left ankle.

4. You now have him locked. Push on your right leg and pull on your left leg.

FRONT KICK-ROUNDHOUSE KICK-SPINNING BACK KICK

1. Start in a fighting stance.

2. Shoot a front kick to the stomach.

3. Plant your foot.

4. Shoot a roundhouse kick to the stomach, using your shin.

Front Kick-Roundhouse Kick-Spinning Back Kick

5. Plant your foot and pivot.

6. End with a back kick to the stomach.

FRONT BALL KICK-HEEL THRUST-LEFT CROSS-ROUNDHOUSE KICK

1. Start in a fighting stance.

2. Execute a quick shuffle.

3. Shoot a front ball kick . . .

4. Plant your foot . . .

5. Deliver a front heel thrust to the jaw,

6. Plant your foot . . .

7. Throw a left cross . . .

8. And end with a roundhouse kick.

FRONT KICK-SIDE KICK-SPINNING BACK KICK

1. Start in a fighting stance.

2. Shoot a front thrust kick . . .

3. Plant your foot . . .

4. Execute a side kick with your left leg . . .

5. Spin . . .

6. And finally, execute a back kick with your right leg.

SIDE KICK-SPINNING BACK KICK-ROUNDHOUSE KICK

1. Start in a fighting stance.

2. Shuffle forward . . .

3. Execute a side kick . . .

4. And land with back feet close together, body turned.

5. Spin . . .

6. And deliver a back kick . . .

7. Spin clockwise on your right foot . . .

8. And end with a roundhouse kick.

SWEEP-ROUNDHOUSE KICK

1. Start in a fighting stance.

2. Turn your body to the left.

3. Kick your opponent in the back of the calf.

4. Twist your body and dip.

5. Rise and look over your left shoulder.

6. Deliver a kick to the head.

ROUNDHOUSE COMBINATIONS

1. Start in a fighting stance.

2. Deliver a power sweep to the back of the calf.

3. Plant your foot back.

4. Shoot a leg kick to the thigh.

5. Plant your foot back.

6. Finish with a high roundhouse to the head.

FRONT KICK-SPINNING WHEEL KICK

1. Start in a fighting stance.

2. Pivot . . .

3. And shoot a front kick.

4. Plant your foot in front of you on its toes.

5. Spin counterclockwise and dip.

6. Rise and deliver a wheel kick to the head. Use your heel.

FRONT KICK-SPINNING BACK KICK

1. Start in a fighting stance.

2. Turn your body forward.

3. Execute a front thrust kick with the right leg.

4. Pivot and plant your foot.

5. Look over your shoulder . . .

6. And deliver a back kick.

FRONT CRESCENT KICK-BACK ROUNDHOUSE SWEEP-SPINNING WHEEL KICK

1. Start in a fighting stance.

2. Bring your back leg to the front leg.

3. Raise your left knee.

4. Deliver a front crescent kick.

5. Plant your feet close.

6. Move your right leg back . . .

7. And deliver a back roundhouse sweep

8. Turn your body and plant your foot on its toes.

9. Spin, looking over your left shoulder.

10. Execute a spinning wheel kick with your heel.

SWITCH FRONT BALL KICK-JUMP SPINNING BACK KICK

1. Start in a fighting stance.

2. Switch your feet without moving your body. Cover your opponent's eyes with your left palm.

3. Execute a front thrust.

4. Plant your foot close to your other foot and dip your body.

5. Spin and jump, lifting your right leg.

6. Deliver a back kick.

POWER ROUNDHOUSE KICK, WITH THE FRONT LEG

1. Start in a fighting stance.

2. Rotate your back shoulder forward.

3. Your rear leg comes up and delivers a kick across the belt line.

4. Return to the starting position.

TECHNIQUES IN MOTION

HOW DO YOU USE TECHNIQUES IN MOTION?

You must have a set pattern that you go through. An example might be front ball kick/roundhouse kick/side kick/punch-punch. That can be your first set routine. Then work out several other routines and practice with a partner while he's holding a bag or sparring. You practice with him while always going in a forward motion. You can't use this pattern going backwards unless it is with a defensive motion.

IS IT BETTER TO RUSH WITH YOUR HANDS OR FEET FIRST?

If your opponent is close to you, it is better to use your hands first and then follow with your feet. If he is at a distance then it is better to use your feet first to close the gap,then use your hands.

IS JAMMING DANGEROUS?

Jamming isn't dangerous if your opponent is about to throw a technique and you jam his weapons because this will throw his timing off. If he isn't throwing a technique, then it is a dangerous move.

WHAT IS THE BEST TECHNIQUE TO USE AFTER JAMMING YOUR OPPONENT?

If all of your weapons are smothered because of jamming, it is better to throw your opponent. A throw can also be a sweep.

HOW DO YOU GO ABOUT TYING UP AN OPPONENT?

First you have to be in close contact with your opponent to tie up his hands. You accomplish this by rushing your opponent and then pressing your forearms against his hands and body. You don't have to worry about his feet because if you have his hands tied, your body is too close for him to kick.

IS IT BETTER TO MOVE AWAY FROM AN ATTACKING OPPONENT OR STAND AND FIGHT?

It is always better to move because if you remain stationary you become a sitting duck. The way you move is in a clockwise or a counterclockwise motion, never in a straight line.

WHAT DO YOU FEEL IS THE MOST EFFECTIVE BLOCK IN KARATE?

To block without blocking is most effective. To redirect. If you have no choice and he kicks low, block with your legs. If he kicks or hits high, tuck your head into your arms. Never reach for his weapons. The idea is to take the impact against your body. If you attempt to block in the traditional manner by raising your arm up, or lowering it down to block a kick, you just leave an opening for your opponent. Any time you use a weapon for a defense, you leave a hole for him to attack.

SHOULD EVERY BLOCK BE FOLLOWED BY A COUNTER ATTACK?

Yes. You should never block-block-block. If you do, your opponent will ultimately wear you down and hurt you. The more you block, the more he takes out of you. The idea is to strike without getting hit. But if you have to take a blow, then make sure you give one.

IS IT HELPFUL TO STUDY JUDO IN CONJUNCTION WITH KARATE?

Knowledge is power. The more you know, the better you can become. Judo teaches you how to fall, and it gives you that inner strength you need. It also makes you very aware of keeping your opponent off balance and how to use his weight against him.

HOW EFFECTIVE ARE TECHNIQUES THAT ARE DONE FROM THE GROUND?

In competition, the fight ends on the ground. In the street, the fight seldom ends on the ground; the fight ends when one of you cah't continue. Martial arts such as aikido and judo have many techniques for the ground which encompass pressure locks, joint locks and chokes.

ARE SPINNING CRESCENT KICKS AND SWEEP KICKS DONE FROM THE GROUND EFFECTIVE IN COMPETITION?

Yes, they are. You can use them in two ways. You can knock your opponent off balance or you can use them to do damage.

WHAT DO YOU THINK ARE THE MOST IMPORTANT THINGS TO KNOW ABOUT TECHNIQUES IN MOTION?

There are three important things to know: your eye gap, your distancing and your timing.

ARE SWEEPS REALLY EFFECTIVE?

Sweeps are very effective. They not only knock your opponent off balance, but they can also do damage.

HOW DO YOU DEVELOP TECHNIQUES FOR CLOSING THE GAP?

To close the gap you have to either fake or feint. You fake with your body and feint with your head. You fake to make him begin a motion, and you feint to keep him on his toes. Once you get him to commit to a motion, there is no turning back. When he begins his technique, you can then smother him.

There is also another technique which is quite effective. You use a slight bounce while you slowly advance in a forward shuffling motion. His eyes will follow your up and down motion and he won't notice that you are closing the distance of the gap.

FRONT KICK-RIGHT CROSS

1. Start in a fighting stance.

2. Twist your body to the right.

3. Raise your knee . . .

4. And deliver a kick.

5. Plant your foot back . . .

6. And deliver a right cross.

FRONT KICK-LEFT HOOK

1. Start in a fighting stance.

2. Twist your body to the right.

3. Deliver a kick.

4. Plant your foot back . . .

5. Twist your shoulders to the left . . .

6. And deliver a left hook.

JAB-DRAG FRONT KICK-RIGHT CROSS-LEFT HOOK

1. Start in a fighting stance.

2. Jab with your left hand. At the same time, drag your right foot up to your left foot.

3. Deliver a front kick to the stomach.

4. Plant your foot forward. Deliver a right cross . . .

5. And a left hook.

FRONT KICK-RIGHT CROSS-LEFT HOOK-RIGHT CROSS

1. Start in a fighting stance.

2. Deliver a kick.

3. Plant your foot back.

4. Deliver a right cross.

5. Plant your foot back.

6. Deliver a left hook . . .

7. And finish with a right cross.

SWITCH JAB-FRONT KICK-UPPER CUT-LEFT HOOK-RIGHT CROSS

1. Start in a fighting stance.

2. Switch your feet and jab.

3. Deliver a kick . . .

4. Plant forward and dip forward . . .

5. Deliver an upper cut . . .

6. Then a left hook . . .

7. And finish with a right cross.

RIGHT CROSS-FRONT KICK-SPINNING BACK KICK

1. Start in a fighting stance.

2. Deliver a right cross to the head.

3. Plant your foot back . . .

4. And kick to the body.

5. Plant your foot back, facing your opponent straight on.

6. Pivot . . .

7. And deliver a back kick.

1. Start in a fighting stance.

2. Deliver a left jab to the head . . .

3. Follow with a roundhouse sweep to his calf.

4. Plant your foot back and dip.

5. Deliver a high whipping roundhouse kick to the head.

ROUNDHOUSE KICK-WINGING RIGHT-ROUNDHOUSE KICK

1. Start in a fighting stance.

2. Raise your knee for a roundhouse kick.

3. Deliver a roundhouse kick to the outside of the opponent's upper arm.

4. Plant your foot back.

5. Shoot a winging right to the kidney.

6. Plant your foot back.

7. Place your right hand on your opponent's head, pressing down.

8. Plant your left foot back and replace your right hand with your left hand on the opponent's head.

9. Dip . . .

10. And deliver a power roundhouse kick to the body.

1. Start in a fighting stance.

2. Deliver a left jab to the face, leaning your body forward.

3. Draw back . . .

4. And deliver a skipping side kick to the body.

5. Pivot and plant your foot close to the right foot.

6. Back kick with the right foot, looking over your right shoulder.

7. Plant your foot next to the left foot, looking over your left shoulder.

8. Back kick with the left foot.

JAB-INSIDE SWEEP-BACK HAND-SPINNING BACK KNUCKLE

1. Start in a fighting stance.

2. Throw a left jab to the face.

3. Cross over.

4. Deliver an inside sweep.

5. Cock your left arm . . .

6. Then deliver a back hand blow to the face.

7. Look over your right shoulder and cock your right arm.

8. Pivot and arc your right arm around, palm out, delivering a back knuckle to the face.

LEFT HOOK-RIGHT HOOK-POWER ROUNDHOUSE KICK-SPINNING BACK KICK

1. Start in a fighting stance.

2. Dip and rotate your right shoulder forward.

Left Hook-Right Hook-Power Roundhouse Kick-Spinning Back Kick

3. Deliver a left hook . . .

4. Then a right hook . . .

5. And a power roundhouse kick to the belt line.

6. Plant your foot back . . .

7. Pivot . . .

8. And finish with a back kick.

FAKE FRONT KICK-RIGHT JAB -LEFT CROSS-FRONT KICK

1. Start in a fighting stance.

2. Lift your right knee.

3. Throw a right jab.

4. Plant your foot forward . . .

5. And deliver a left cross.

6. Finish with a front kick.

JAB-SKIPPING INSIDE SWEEP-RIGHT CROSS-POWER ROUND-HOUSE KICK

1. Start in a fighting stance.

2. Deliver a left hand jab.

3. Skip forward and lift your leg at the knee.

4. Deliver an inside sweep below the calf.

5. Continue with a right cross.

6. Finish with a power roundhouse to the body.

JAB-THRUSTING HEEL KICK-ROUNDHOUSE KICK

1. Start in a fighting stance.

2. Throw a left hand jab as you drag your right foot forward.

3. Deliver a thrusting heel kick to the face.

4. Plant your foot.

5. Put your right leg back.

6. Deliver a roundhouse kick to the thigh.

Jab-Thrusting Heel Kick-Roundhouse Kick

7. Plant your foot back and dip.

8. Finish with a roundhouse kick to the head.

JAB-FAKE SIDE KICK-JUMPING SPINNING BACK KICK

1. Start in a fighting stance.

2. Throw a left jab.

3. Pull back and lift your left knee while pivoting to the right.

4. Plant your foot.

5. Jump and spin.

6. Deliver a back kick to the opponent's body.

UPWARD HEAD BUTT (ALLOWED IN THE ORIENT)

1. Start in a fighting stance.

2. When your opponent jabs, weave underneath.

3. Put your head into the opponent's solar plexus.

4. Lock your knees and lift your head, clipping the opponent on the chin.

FORWARD HEAD BUTT (ALLOWED IN THE ORIENT)

1. Start in a fighting stance.

2. When your opponent throws a left jab, you parry it.

3. Begin to move forward, dipping low and putting your head almost next to his chest.

4. Deliver a head butt by rising up and forward into the opponent's face.

SIDE HEAD BUTT (ALLOWED IN THE ORIENT)

1. Start in a fighting stance.

2. When your opponent jabs, parry his blow.

3. Move into a clinch position, with your head on his left shoulder.

4. Slide your head over, clipping your opponent's jaw.

5. Do not stop when you clip his jaw, but follow through.

6. Come back the opposite way, clipping him again.

HEAD THROW

1. Start in a fighting stance.

2. When your opponent jabs, you weave.

Head Throw

3. Rush in and put your arms over his arms.

4. Clinch, keeping your head low so he can't head butt you.

5. Wrap your left arm around his neck.

6. Turn your body 180 degrees . . .

7. And pull him over your hip.

8. Once he has landed, follow through with a technique if it is allowed in the rules. Remember: There are no rules on the street.

OUTSIDE FOOT THROW

1. Start in a fighting stance.

2. Your opponent jabs.

3. Put your right leg on the outside of his left leg as you clinch.

4. Fall backwards as you twist to your right.

5. Don't allow him to fall on top of you.

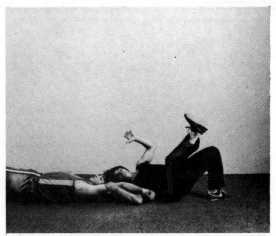

6. Complete the technique.

INSIDE FOOT TRIP

1. Clinch, keeping your head to your opponent's shoulder.

2. Place your right foot outside of the opponent's left leg.

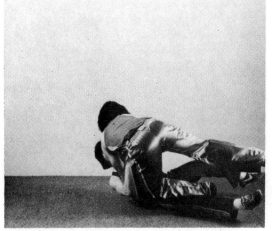

3. Roll to your right side, pulling him down.

4. Land, keeping his left elbow locked.

5. Roll over on top of him.

6. Follow through.

HIP THROW

1. Start in a fighting stance.

2. When your opponent jabs, parry his blow.

3. Clinch, keeping your head low so he can't head butt you.

4. Wrap your left arm around his waist.

5. Throw him over your hip and leg.

COORDINATION

HOW WOULD YOU DEFINE COORDINATION?

Coordination is making your weapons work as one, such as working hands and feet together in combinations.

IS THE SPEED BAG A PRACTICAL METHOD OF LEARNING HAND COORDINATION?

Yes, it gives you a different kind of coordination. It gives you coordination in working the hands. It coordinates the body to move either with the bag, away from the bag or from side to side.

WHAT IS MEANT BY EYE GAP COORDINATION?

Your eye determines a certain distance which you coordinate with your weapons. Your eye then catches any additional gap created by your opponent's movement. You have to then alter your technique which is already in motion. An example would be, you start out with a hand technique and in the middle of the move your opponent moves out of range. You catch this additional gap in distance so you change your tactics from your original technique to one that will bridge that gap.

DOES TIMING HAVE ANYTHING TO DO WITH COORDINATION?

Yes, it does. By your opponent moving in a certain direction, you have to be able to judge the time it would take to use a weapon with a technique and the length of time it would take to make contact.

WHAT ARE SOME METHODS OF DEVELOPING COORDINATION?

Jumping rope helps you coordinate your hands and feet. Other aids include your speed bag and timing bag.

CAN ONE DEVELOP COORDINATION OR DOES ONE HAVE TO BE BORN WITH IT?

When you are doing something new it's natural to feel uncoordinated. Coordination definitely can be developed.

IS KATA TRAINING GOOD FOR COORDINATION?

Yes. In fact, it is one of the most popular methods of training your body because you are kicking and striking and moving your body in many different directions. It certainly is a good training device for coordination.

WHAT IS THE CONCEPT OF MAKING YOUR WEAPONS WORK AS ONE?

Whenever you train, whether shadow boxing or working with the bag, always use both your hands and feet during that work-out. In that way, you can practice making your weapons work in one continuous movement when you throw combinations. You will get into the habit of making them work as one and that will carry over into actual competition. The way you train is the way you react.

WHIRLWIND

1. Hold both hands in front of you, arms bent.

2. Begin to rotate your hands around each other.

3. Continue the circular movement.

4. Continue the arc in a smooth steady movement.

5. Once completed, begin again.

WINDMILL

1. Face forward in a horse stance. Both palms face forward, and thumbs are touching.

2. Begin moving your palms in a circle counter to each other.

3. Continue the circular movement.

4. Complete the circle and begin again.

1. Face forward. One arm is up; the other is down.

2. Twist your body to your right.

3. Dip, palms out.

4. Face forward. One palm faces left; the other faces right. Both are going in the same clockwise direction.

5. Twist your body to the left. Your hands are now going in a counterclockwise direction.

6. Continue that movement until you pivot your body to the right and repeat.

SIMULTANEOUS PUNCHING

1. Face your partner, with both fists high in the chamber.

2. Your partner holds up his hands as shown, and you punch both hands at the same time.

3. Pull your hands back. Your partner changes his hand position. Punch both hands again.

4. Pull your hands back. Your partner changes his hand position. Punch both hands at the same time again.

5. Pull back again. Your partner changes his hand position. (They can even be crossed as shown in the photo.)

FOREARM SWING

1. Bring your left fist up, with arm bent 90 degrees, right fist in the chamber.

2. As your right fist punches, your left fist moves behind the shoulder.

3. Move your left arm in an arc for an inward block, right fist in the chamber.

4. Punch out with your right fist. Your left fist moves at the same time behind the shoulder. After working your right side 20 times, do the same routine with the opposite side.

DOWNWARD BLOCKS

1. Face your partner, with both hands in the chamber.

2. Both you and your partner put your left arms to the opposite side as shown.

3. Make contact in a downward block.

4. Raise the opposite arms.

5. Make contact in a downward block.

6. Raise opposite arms and repeat the exercise a minimum of 20 times.

HAND SLAP

1. You will recognize this game you played as a kid. Here's your chance to play it again. Take the starting position.

2. Try to slap your opponent's hands.

3. Speed and reflex are used in this exercise.

4. Never look at the hands. Learn to read your opponent's face and you can tell when he will make his move.

SLAP TRAINING

1. Start in a fighting stance.

2. When your opponent throws a punch, parry his left hand. At the same time, move your opposite hand toward his face, slapping it gently.

3. Your opponent throws another punch. Parry that punch . . .

4. And slap his face gently.

ANKLE SWEEPS

1. Take the starting position, with feet flat on the floor and both arms out to your side.

2. Hop on the left foot.

3. Let the momentum swing your right foot out.

4. Hop on your right foot.

5. Let the momentum swing your left foot out.

6. Hop back on your left foot kicking your right foot out. Complete the cycle. Do a minimum of 20 times.

LEG-HAND COORDINATION

1. Take the starting position.

2. Pull your left leg back, and put both hands out to the right.

3. Pull your left knee up, and pull both hands in to your left side.

4. Hop over to the opposite foot and extend your hands out to your left.

5. Bring your right knee up, bringing both hands down to the right.

6. Hop over to the opposite foot, and extend your hands to the right.

RUSSIAN HOP

1. Squat down on your toes. Have a partner hold your hand for support if needed.

2. Kick out both legs.

3. Bring them back before you land.

4. Land in balance.

RUSSIAN KICKOUT

1. Squat down on your toes. Have a partner hold your hand for support if needed.

2. Kick out the left foot.

3. Kick out the right foot.

4. Kick out the left foot.

FLUTTER KICK-ARM CIRCLE COMBINATION

1. Sit on the floor, arms straight out, legs six inches off the ground.

2. Flutter kick your legs while making circles with your arms.

3. Continue flutter kicking, making the circles larger and then smaller.

COORDINATED JUMPING JACKS

1. Take the starting position.

2. Open . . .

3. And cross . . .

4. Open . . .

5. And cross . . .

6. Open (and cross, with rhythm).

DOUBLE UP-JUMPING JACKS

1. Face your partner, holding hands.

2. Open . . .

3. And cross . . .

4. Open . . .

5. And cross . . .

6. Open (and cross, with rhythm).

SEE-SAW

1. Hold your partner's hands. Your left hand and left leg are forward.

2. Jump and switch . . .

3. Land . . .

4. Jump and switch. Repeat a minimum of 20 times.

SHOULDER TAP

1. Start in a fighting stance.

2. Your opponent throws a jab, trying to hit your shoulder.

3. You pivot out of the way.

4. Return to a fighting stance.

DISTANCING DRILLS

1. Start in a fighting stance.

2. Place your left hand on his forehead.

3. Pivot out of the way.

4. Place your hand on his forehead, keeping him out of the way.

THE SUMO TOUCH

1. Face your opponent in Sumo position, hands by your side.

2. Try to touch your opponent's thigh as he tries to block you.

3. Alternate your hands.

4. Take turns in attacking.

5. Learn to read your opponent's face.

6. Repeat.

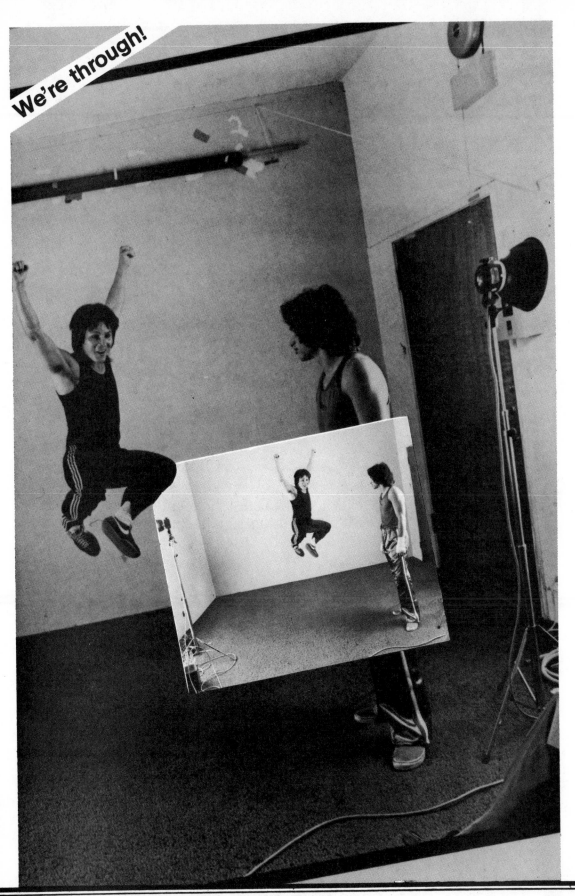

Listening Creates Reflex.   Just as a blind man learns to use his ears to react to noise, so must you train yourself to listen, to become aware, to respond automatically.

Balance: Centering Your Weight In Yourself.   You should always have your weight centered in yourself because only then will you have natural balance.

Good Posture Creates Good Vision and Focus.   To be able to look at your opponent properly from shoulder to shoulder, you must maintain a good posture at all times. Otherwise, your image and focus will be distorted and your judgment will be inaccurate.

The Way You Train Is The Way You React.   Train hard in your workouts and you will fight hard in the ring. Don't pull your punches or kicks while you are training and you won't pull them in the ring or in the street.

Coordination: Making Your Weapons Work As One.   Train both your hands and feet together. Only then will they work as one coordinated weapon.

Self-Confidence: Knowing You Can Do It Even Though You've Never Tried.   You must believe in yourself and your ability. If something new or unexpected is required of you, do it without hesitation. Without self-confidence, you have nothing.

Never move back. If you must move back always do so in a clockwise or counterclockwise direction. Never move back in a straight line.

Never set yourself in one spot. Always move around. Make it difficult for your opponent to plan an attack.

Redirect. Never allow your opponent to attack you head on. Always redirect his attacking weapons so that you minimize his offense.

Fight your opponent the way he fights you. Show him that you're better than he is on all levels. That will make him less sure of his own ability.

Place your opponent where you want him. Do this by testing his reactions. Based on this, set him up with faking and feinting techniques. Then go in for the knockout.

- Never change what works.
- Grasp whatever you can, be open-minded about everything.
- Learn what you want to learn, but never close your mind to something different.
- Knowing yourself helps you to know others.
- Never stop learning, never limit yourself to what you think you may attain.
- To be in 100 percent physical shape you must first be in 100 percent mental shape.
- Respect your judgment. Remember, you cannot fool yourself.
- Take defeat as a process of learning.
- Never degrade yourself by thinking negatively.
- If you lose, figure out why you lost and find the defenses which will help you the next time.
- In and out of the ring the secret of a martial artist is to control his anger.
- There is no time for being old-fashioned. One must progress.
- Learn to train your mind to be ahead of your body.
- Beat the pain mentally and you can go on forever.
- Don't try to be just as good as somebody else; strive to be better.
- The way you train is the way you react.

EMIL FARKAS was born in Hungary. Before reaching the age of twenty he earned his black belt in both judo and karate. He is the owner of the Beverly Hills Karate Academy. Today he's known and respected internationally as a coach and teacher to major movie and television actors, actresses, and stunt men. In addition, Emil has appeared in over ten features and dozens of television shows as an actor, stunt man, and fight choreographer. His previous books include *The Complete Martial Arts Catalogue, Fight Back—A Woman's Guide To Self Defense, The Martial Arts Dictionary;* and *The World Martial Arts Encyclopedia.* As a screenwriter, Emil has written the original screenplay for *Force: Five,* starring world champions Joe Lewis, Benny Urquidez and Bong Soo Han. He is also a regular columnist for *Inside Kung-Fu, Kick Illustrated,* and *Official Karate* magazines. He is the founder and president of Creative Action, Inc., a multifaceted company dealing with management, promotion, and motion picture production.

STUART SOBEL was born in North Carolina and moved to California as a youngster. He graduated from college with a degree in business. In 1970 he began his study of karate under Emil Farkas. Since then Stuart has continued to pursue the martial arts, not just in the dojo, but in the realm of the business world as well. In 1975 he became executive vice president of Creative Action, Inc. Among his many endeavors, he manages the career of world karate champion Benny Urquidez. In addition, he is a top freelance writer and photographer. His articles have been featured in every major martial arts publication in the United States. Currently living in Beverly Hills with his lovely wife Eleanor, he continues his study of the Oriental martial arts.

ABOUT THE AUTHOR

Born in 1952 in the heart of the barrios of Los Angeles, Benny Urquidez was the second youngest in a family of nine. His father was a professional boxer and his mother a professional wrestler, so his fighting blood came naturally.

After competing in boxing as a child, he began his life-long study of the martial arts at the age of eight. Arnold Urquidez, the eldest brother, was his first and most influential instructor. However, he also studied under such masters as Ed Parker, Tak Kubota, Bill Ryusaki and Clarence Akuda. By age 14, the young karateka received his black belt. He began to formulate his own unique style which he terms "free form." This fierce competitor was a constant winner in tournament competition.

An extremely colorful fighter, he captivated audiences in England and Belgium as a member of Ed Parker's 1974 United States team. When professional karate emerged during that same year, Urquidez retired from traditional competition. He became part of the National Karate League (N.K.L.) and fought on their Southern California-based team, the L.A. Stars. Eventually he quit fighting for that team and began fighting for himself. Having fought under the sanctioning bodies of the N.K.L., the World Karate Association (W.K.A.), the Professional Karate Association (P.K.A.); for Aaron Banks and Tommy Lee, he always emerged with their respective world titles. He was given the nickname of "The Jet" during a bout in New York by some enthusiastic fans early in his career. The name stuck.

He continued to fight as well as spearhead full-contact karate in the United States. In 1977, he traveled to Japan where he defeated the best kick boxers that country had to offer. He currently holds both the lightweight and super lightweight world titles. He has a record of over fifty undefeated title bouts to date.

Benny has been featured in two films, both documentaries on the martial arts. Produced by the late Elvis Presley and still unreleased, *The New Gladiators* deals with tournament competition. The second documentary was produced and released in Japan, where it was a box-office smash. This film shows the professional side of the fighting arts. Titled *Kings of the Square Ring*, it also features Muhammad Ali and Antonio Inoki.

The Jet's fights have been televised on all of the major networks in the United States and Japan as well as worldwide through distribution to our military bases via American Armed Forces Radio and Television Service. He has also appeared on numerous talk shows, among them the *Merv Griffin* and *Mike Douglas* programs.

Inside Kung-Fu magazine says, "Benny Urquidez emerges as the brightest star on karate's pro circuit." *Official Karate* magazine states, "He is a technician in the science of fighting. The king of the hill." In 1978, *Black Belt* magazine voted him "Fighter of the Year" and placed him in *Black Belt's* Hall of Fame.

Living in Tarzana, California with his wife Sara and daughter Monique, he is constantly traveling the globe either fighting or instructing. The champ will soon be opening the ultimate martial arts center in Los Angeles. He is currently starring in the film, *Force: Five,* with Joe Lewis and Bong Soo Han. Benny Urquidez is certainly jet-propelled inside and out of the ring.

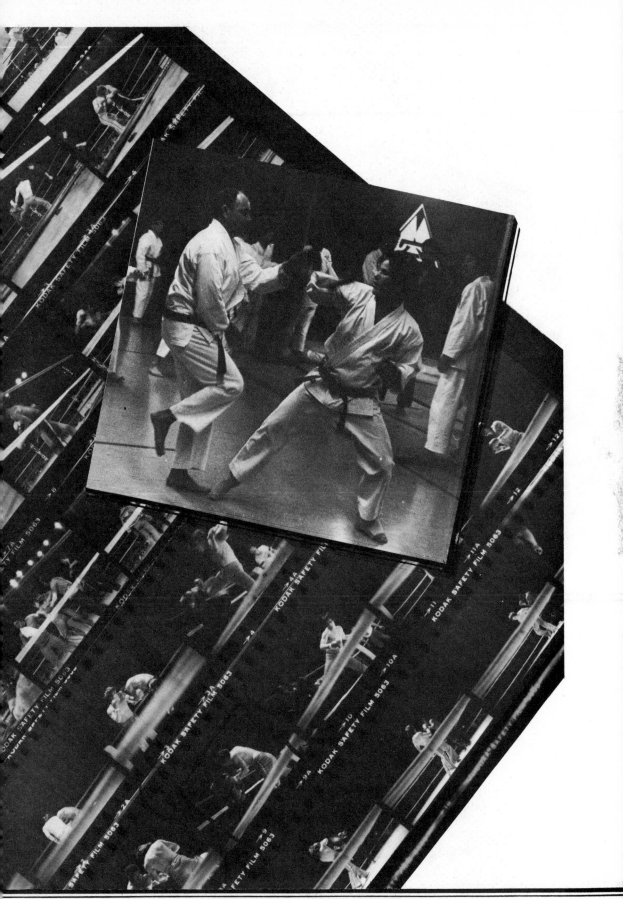